DUNAMIS!
Power From On High!

Receiving the Baptism in the Holy Spirit & Fire!

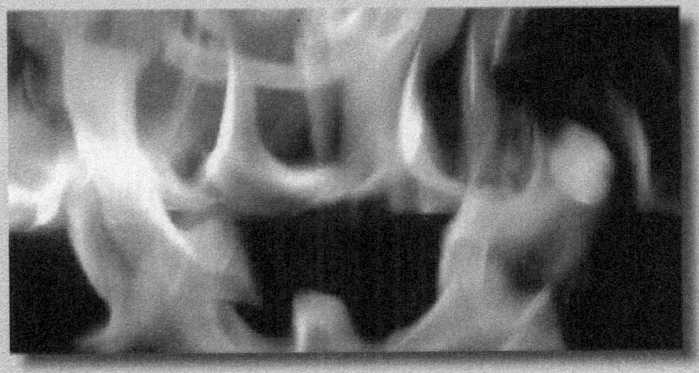

STEVEN LAMBERT
ThD, DMin

Unless otherwise indicated, Scripture quotations are from The *New American Standard Bible*, copyright © 1960, 1962, 1963, 1968, 1971, 1972, 1973, 1975, 1977, 1988; The Lockman Foundation. All rights reserved. Used by permission.

Scripture quotations marked AB are from the *Amplified Bible*, Old Testament © 1965, 1987 by the Zondervan Corporation; *The Amplified New Testament* © 1958, 1987 by the Lockman Foundation. Used by permission.

Scripture quotations marked KJV are from the *King James Verson* of the Bible. Public domain.

DUNAMIS! POWER FROM ON HIGH!

© Copyright 2012; Steven Lambert, ThD, DMin. All rights reserved under International Copyright Law. Contents and/or cover in whole or part may not be reproduced, stored in any electronic retrieval system, transmitted in any form by any means—mechanical, electronic, photocopying, recording, or otherwise—without prior written permission of the author. Published by:

Real Truth Publications
P.O. Box 911
Jupiter, FL 33468-0911
Email: admin@realtruthpublications.com
Website: www.realtruthpublications.com

ISBN 978-1-887915-05-2 (Print Version)
ISBN 978-1-887915-11-3 (PDF Ebook Version)
ISBN 978-1-887915-13-7 (Epub Version)
ISBN 978-1-887915-14-4 (Kindle Version)

Printed in the United States of America.

Contents

Foreword By Charles Carrin 5

Introduction 6

Chapter 1: Overview 9

Chapter 2: Born From On High 12

Chapter 3: Jesus—The Baptizer in the Holy Spirit 17

Chapter 4: The Spirit's Work in Regeneration 27

Chapter 5: The Spirit's Work in Spirit-Baptism 33

Chapter 6: Tongues—The Initial Evidence 54

Chapter 7: The Pauline Example 73

Chapter 8: The Samarian Example 96

Chapter 9: The Gentile Example 101

Chapter 10: The Ephesian Example 108

Chapter 11: The Early Church Example 116

Chapter 12: The Charismata 125

Chapter 13: Tongues & Interpretation of Tongues .. 138

Chapter 14: Cessationism Refuted 152

Chapter 15: A Different Gospel—Void of Power 162

Chapter 16: Receiving the Baptism in the Holy Spirit 176

A Special Invitation

Believer in Christ, have you been praying for Divine intervention or God's help in real, overwhelming needs in your life?

Jesus told the early disciples that it was expedient for them that He "go away," for when He did, He would send the Holy Spirit, the Helper, to them to act and speak on His behalf and in His stead. Then He promised them they would receive POWER (*dunamis*, Greek) after the Holy Spirit had come upon them, which He did on the Day of Pentecost, and they did—i.e., receive power when the Holy Spirit came upon them.

Jesus' promise He made to those early disciples was extended to *every* disciple since the time He originally made it, and multiplied millions have received it as well.

Have you asked Jesus to immerse and envelop you in the power of the Holy Spirit?

The same power that He operated in to heal the sick, cleanse lepers, cast out demons, raise the dead, and perform mighty miracles is available to you *today* through the same Baptism in the Spirit that He Himself received as a model to us all.

The message contained in the pages of this book can revolutionize your life, as you learn how to be clothed with *dunamis-power* from on High!

FOREWORD
BY CHARLES CARRIN

Steven Lambert brings to the conference table a unique combination of scholarly insight into Scripture and an intense prophetic voice. I personally know of no one else who carries this combination as well as he. His writing skills are equal to his theological intellect.

It is apparent that his concern is for Biblical truth—regardless of which camp has it—and he allows no religious bias to distort that pursuit. Dr. Lambert is not only fair-minded with those who differ from him regarding the topic at hand, but equally demanding of himself in presenting his own view. That determination wonderfully permeates the entirety of this book. That, coupled with his wide overview of Christian history gives him qualifications beyond many others.

What I am saying is this: I learned from this book. You will too. Time spent in this study will not be wasted. Even if you already hold opinions different to the writer, the challenge will be profoundly beneficial to you.

You will find the book well-organized, and that topics move progressively in an easy-to-follow way. I found Chapters Three, Four, and Five—that present the successive works of Jesus and the Holy Spirit—to be very concise and logical. They are not "mystique" but analytic, precise, to the point.

You will be benefitted in two ways by this volume: *Theologically*, you will be better <u>informed</u>. *Logistically*, you will be better <u>trained</u>. That means the reading experience itself is beneficial. As you explore the book you will understand what I mean. Read on!

Charles Carrin, Pastor Emeritus
(February 12, 2014, Boynton Beach, FL)

INTRODUCTION

What you hold in your hands is not merely a book—it is a journey! The journey's destination is the *Real Truth* about a matter second in importance to none, next to salvation itself—*the Baptism in the Holy Spirit*! God calls it "Dunamis-Power from on High (Heaven)!" Each chapter of this volume is a vital leg of the journey, leading ultimately to irrefutable truth concerning the role of the Third Member of the Godhead, whom Jesus Himself called, "The Helper"—the Precious Holy Spirit, the Living Waters of God.

Long ago, God declared through a prophet named Hosea that HIS people—that means Born Again believers, Christians—are *destroyed* for lack of knowledge (Hos. 4:6)! Spiritual ignorance, or lack of knowledge concerning spiritual matters, not only is not bliss, but it is an open gateway to devastation, defeat, and destruction. Jesus taught that *knowledge* of the Truth is what sets genuine disciples free (Jn. 8:31-32), which inherently means that what you do *not* know of the Truth will keep you reeling in bondage and confinement. Indeed, the unfortunate truth is that many Born Again believers are being held captive by lack of knowledge of the Truth and deceptions concerning this critical matter of the Baptism of the Holy Spirit and Fire!

The two main points I will be establishing with Scriptural support repeatedly throughout this book are that: 1) The *Baptism* in the Holy Spirit is a separate and distinct, or adjunctive, experience to the *infusion* of the Holy Spirit that takes place at the moment of salvation; and, 2) *regeneration* by the *infusion* of Spirit (i.e., the New Birth, the spiritual transaction that occurs at salvation) and the *immersion* or

Baptism in the Holy Spirit, are two distinct and separate workings of the same Holy Spirit.

In salvation, the Holy Spirit comes to live *within* the believer, imparting the *Fruit* of the Spirit—that is the regenerative work of the Holy Spirit. In the *Baptism* in the Holy Spirit, the believer is *enveloped* by or *immersed* in the Holy Spirit; that is to say, the Holy Spirit comes *upon* the believer, in contrast to *in* the believer, and imparts the *Gifts* (*charismata*, Greek) of the Holy Spirit.

These facts are clearly and irrefutably supported by Scripture, and exemplified by the experience of Jesus Himself, who is our supreme Model. Indeed, the overarching Truth of this book is—*Jesus is the Baptizer in the Holy Spirit*—just as John The Baptist, the original Baptist, testified of Him: "He will baptize you with the Holy Spirit and fire!" (Mat. 3:11).

Jesus explicitly stated that the Baptism in the Holy Spirit will be given to *any* believer who simply *asks* Him for it (Lk. 11:13). The Baptism in the Holy Spirit is a gift of grace received by faith, and often imparted through the laying on of hands by other anointed believers, though that is not required.

Never, in Church history, really Creation history, has the need for the outpouring of the Dunamis-Power of God "upon all flesh" (Joel 2:28; Ac. 2:17) been greater! Global prevalence of deception of the highest order coupled with ubiquitous moral and spiritual decline is what makes the need so desperate and burning.

Deception abounds in this hour—not only in the world, but also within the Church—to such an extent that Jesus' prediction and admonition concerning the prevailing spiritual landscape in the last days that "even the elect" shall be deceived (Mk. 13:22), is no longer just a remote prospect, but an undeniable reality, transpiring right under the proverbial nose of those ecclesiastical entities claiming to be part of the "Church."

The only answer to all the uncertainties and devastations now occurring with unprecedented and mindboggling speed, is the same answer Jesus gave to the question the early disciples asked of Him just prior to His Ascension into Heaven to sit down on His Throne at the right hand of God:

> Gathering them together, He commanded them not to leave Jerusalem, but to wait for what the Father had promised, "Which," He said, "you heard of from Me; for John baptized with water, but you will be baptized with the Holy Spirit not many days from now." So when they had come together, they were asking Him, saying, "Lord, is it at this time You are restoring the kingdom to Israel?" He said to them, "**It is not for you to know times or epochs which the Father has fixed by His own authority; but you will receive power when the Holy Spirit has come upon you; and you shall be My witnesses** both in Jerusalem, and in all Judea and Samaria, and even to the remotest part of the earth." (Ac. 1:4-8)

As Jesus instructed His disciples in the First Century, so also is He instructing His disciples today in the Twenty-First Century: It is not for us to know times or epochs which the Father has fixed by His own authority, for knowing those things will not empower us to live the abundant and victorious life Jesus came to give us (Jn. 10:10). Rather, what we need to live that "zoe-life" of God is the Dunamis-Power that we will receive when the Holy Spirit has come upon us, in order to be His triumphant and overcoming witnesses both in our local area of residence and function (Jerusalem), and translocally—i.e., in the more extended regions beyond our locality, as well as our nation (Judea and Samaria), and globally—"even to the remotest part of the earth." And, that power is received and activated in our lives when we receive the Baptism in the Holy Spirit and Fire from Jesus, the Baptizer in the Holy Spirit!

Chapter One
Overview

Reader, you are about to fulfill your destiny, with this divinely-appointed divine encounter with the Third Member of the Godhead, the Living Waters of God, and with the *Real Truth* regarding this absolutely vital matter of the Baptism in the Holy Spirit. This issue is so critical to every believer's walk with the Lord that it is undeniably the one issue that your adversary the Devil has continued to fight tooth and nail, and do all he can to hinder and, if possible, preclude believers from receiving since that fateful day when Jesus Himself, the original Prototype of the Sons of God, was baptized in the Holy Spirit, wherein the Holy Spirit descended upon Him in the form of a Dove, as a visible sign of testimony identifying Him as the long-awaited Messiah.

In the two-plus millennia that have transpired since, no other single issue has been more controversial, fiercely debated, and bitterly divisive in the annals of church history. And, that should not be at all surprising because the last thing on Earth that Satan wants is people to know the *Real Truth* regarding the inexhaustible and uncontainable power that is made available to every believer who receives of this same baptism that the original Baptist, John the Baptist, freely admitted that he needed to receive from Jesus, and the same baptism with which our ultimate Model in all spiritual things Himself received, and which elicited the divine response out of the Heavenlies, "This is My Beloved Son in whom I am well-pleased!" (Mat. 3:17).

Friends of God, if you have even the slightest desire to be well-pleasing to God, there is no other way to achieve that place of standing with our Heavenly Father than to follow in the path laid by the Heavenly Model, who came to Earth as a Man, and likewise receive of this indescribable gift of the Baptism in the Holy Spirit.

Jesus commanded the early disciples to wait in Jerusalem for "the promise of the Father" (Ac. 1:4), which He specified was that they would "be baptized in the Holy Spirit not many days from now" (Ac. 1:5), meaning not many days from the day He appeared to them and spoke those words just prior to His final ascension into Heaven to claim His seat of sovereignty at the right hand of God. That commandment has continued to reverberate through the more than two-thousand years that have transpired since, unto every disciple of Jesus who has made that decision to accept Jesus as their personal Lord and Savior and be Born Again by the regenerative work of the same Holy Spirit.

Ten days later, on the Day of Pentecost, the Holy Ghost descended upon the early disciples of Jesus in the form of Spiritual Fire, spread by a rushing mighty wind of the Spirit (Ac. 2:1-3). The Spirit settled upon them as cloven tongues of fire. And they were all filled with the Spirit and began praising and glorifying God in languages unknown to them that they had never before spoken, as the Holy Spirit gave them the utterances—languages and dialects known by those who were witnessing this phenomenal, unprecedented, and undeniable supernatural sign of the outpouring of the Holy Spirit—who came upon this initial harvest of Born Again believers with such power and ecstatic joy that they became inebriated in the Spirit to such an extent that those witnessing this supernatural phenomenon supposed them to be intoxicated with new wine, and began mocking them for their drunken behavior.

Finally, the Apostle Peter, accompanied by the other eleven apostles stood to his feet, probably from a prone position because of having been "slain in the Spirit," and declared to all those who were witnessing this supernatural event that these people who were receiving this outpouring of the Spirit were not drunk with wine as they supposed, but rather, *this* (phenomenon) was *that* of which the prophet Joel had prophesied hundreds of years before—that in the last day God would pour out His Spirit upon all flesh, effecting supernatural results—signs and wonders on the Earth below and in the sky above (Joel 2:28-32).

And what a great story that is! But, the best part of the story is that it has yet to be finished! The ending is still being written by the Holy Spirit yet today. That same Pentecostal outpouring of the Spirit is still flowing yet today, and it is available to every believer in Jesus who decides he or she is sick and tired of being sick and tired and powerless against the never-ending onslaught of an unrelenting enemy of our souls, and bereft of spiritual capacity to bless and be a blessing to others.

It's available to you today, friend, but you must take a step of faith, and follow in the footsteps of the original Baptist—John The Baptist—and tell Jesus you recognize that He is the Baptizer in the Holy Ghost and Fire, and ask Him to baptize, or totally immerse, *you* in the Living Waters of the Spirit of God. He *will* do it, but He testified that you must **ask** Him for the Holy Spirit's baptism:

> "So I say to you, **ASK**, and it will be given to you; seek, and you will find; knock, and it will be opened to you. "For **everyone** **who asks, receives**; and he who seeks, finds; and to him who knocks, it will be opened. "Now suppose one of you fathers is asked by his son for a fish; he will not give him a snake instead of a fish, will he? "Or *if* he is asked for an egg, he will not give him a scorpion, will he? "If you then, being evil, know how to give good gifts to your children, how much more will *your* **heavenly Father give the Holy Spirit to those who ASK Him**?" (Lk. 11:9-13)

Follow along now as we embark on a journey to receive the "dunamis-power" from on high that Jesus promised the early disciples and every disciple since would receive "when the Holy Spirit has come upon you," which will empower the recipient to be His witness "even to the remotest part of the Earth" (Ac. 1:8).

Chapter Two
Born From On High

There is much distortion, misunderstanding, and diverse teaching regarding this matter of the Baptism in the Holy Spirit. But, in this chapter, we're going to start our journey to unravel all of that distortion and confusion, and arrive at the *Real Truth* regarding this absolutely vital matter.

The first point I want to make about this matter is that Jesus was born of the Holy Spirit in a similar way as believers are *born again*. It was not necessary for Jesus to be born *again*, because He was not born of the sin nature as are humans, but of God the Father. And that's an important starting point, because we as believers were born into sin by our natural birth, and then we "must be born again" (Jn. 3:7) in order to be born "from above" as Jesus was already "born"—really in His case *begotten*—from above (cf., Jn. 3:31; 8:23).

The first one is Matthew 1:18-20. The Gospel of Matthew begins by saying, "The book of the genealogy of Jesus Christ, the Son of David, the son of Abraham," and then goes on to list all of the generations that eventually produced Mary, who, as we know, was a young virgin woman who God chose as the human mother to give birth to Jesus. This account in Matthew, in other words, is a delineation of the *maternal* lineage of the Christ.

And then, in verse 18, it says, "Now the *birth* of Jesus Christ was as follows." Notice that this is about the *birth* of Jesus Christ. "When his mother Mary had been betrothed to Joseph before they came together, she was found to be with child by the Holy Spirit." "She was found to be with

Child by the Holy Spirit"—in other words, what this is talking about—as we know, it was what some call "an immaculate conception"—that Jesus was not born through the normal procreation process, rather, at the time when the Holy Spirit overshadowed Mary, the Holy Spirit supernaturally inseminated the womb of Mary with the Divine Seed (*sperma*, Gr.) of the Son of God. So, it says that "she was found to be with Child *by the Holy Spirit.*" This is telling us that both the substance (i.e., the Seed and the resultant Child) and the process were by the Holy Spirit! This was no ordinary birth, but entirely supernatural by the working of the Holy Spirit!

> And Joseph her husband, being a righteous man, and not wanting to disgrace her, desired to put her away secretly, but when he had considered this, behold, an angel of the Lord appeared to him in a dream, saying "Joseph, son of David, do not be afraid to take Mary as your wife, for that which has been conceived in her is *of the Holy Spirit.*" (Mat. 1:19-20)

So, we see that with regards to the *paternal* side of Jesus' fleshly life, He was born "of the Holy Spirit," not as a result of human procreation or seed. Now this is an important point because the way Born Again believers are "born from above" is that we are born again, or spiritually regenerated, i.e., our formerly "dead" human spirit (Eph. 2:1) is regenerated, revived, or reborn from death, through the supernatural working of the Holy Spirit in regeneration.

Remember that Jesus told Nicodemus, "You must be born again!" (Jn. 3:7). And, this is why it is vital that when a person is born again, the transaction that takes place be a *real* regenerative transaction that transpires through the regenerative work of the Holy Spirit. Being born again, it is imperative to understand, is not merely "turning over a new leaf," like a "New Year's resolution." It is not deciding to do better. It is not a resolve to do better. Rather, it is literally our human spirit being reborn, thereby producing "a new creature" in Christ (2 Cor. 5:17). And, like Nicodemus asked of Jesus, "How can I go back into my mother's womb and be born *again*?"—we cannot go back into our mother's womb, and be born *again*. But, Jesus wasn't talking about a physical rebirth; rather a spiritual rebirth. He answered him by saying, "that which is born of the flesh is *flesh*; and that which is born of the Spirit is *spirit*."

When we're truly and literally born again—not simply having walked down a church aisle and shook a preacher's hand—it's not that that makes you born again, it's not joining a church that makes you born again—what makes you born again is receiving the Lord Jesus Christ, sincerely, earnestly praying to receive Him into your heart, believing that God has raised Him from the dead, confessing with your mouth the Lord Jesus Christ as your personal Savior and Lord (Rom. 10:9)—**then** the Bible promises that we are Born Again—in that our *spirit* is *reborn* from spiritual death.

As Jesus said, "That which is born of the Spirit is *spirit*." It's our human *spirit* that is born again when we receive Jesus into our heart. (The words *heart* and *spirit* are interchangeable in Biblical parlance.) And that's the most important point when we begin to study the matter of the *regenerative* work of the Holy Spirit, as compared to the *second* work of the Holy Spirit, which comes in the *Baptism* in the Holy Spirit.

Continuing with our starting point regarding this greatly misunderstood matter of the Baptism in the Holy Spirit, which is that Jesus was born of the Holy Spirit, and so therefore it was not necessary for Him to be "born again" as redeemed human beings are. "*(We)* must be born again" Jesus said (Jn. 3:7). But, it was not necessary for *Him* to be born again, and we already looked at one passage of Scripture that talked about that in Matthew 1:18-20. Now we want to look at one other passage of Scripture as support for that first point I'm making, i.e., Luke 1:26-28:

> Now in the six month the angel Gabriel was sent from God to a city in Galilee, called Nazareth, to a virgin engaged to a man whose name was Joseph, of the descendents of David; and the virgin's name was Mary.

And coming in, he said to her, "Hail favored one! the Lord is with you." But, she was greatly troubled at this statement, and kept pondering what kind of salutation this might be. And, the angel said to her, "Do not be afraid Mary, for you have found favor with God. And, behold, you will conceive in your womb, and bear a son, and you shall name Him Jesus. He will be great, and He will be called the Son of the Most High, and the Lord God will give Him the throne of his father David, and He will reign over the house of Jacob forever; and His kingdom will have no end." And Mary said to the angel, "How can this be, since I am a virgin." And the angel answered and said to her, "The Holy Spirit will come *upon* you, and the power of the most high will *overshadow* you; and for that reason, the Holy Offspring shall be called the Son of God."

Notice that statement! That is such a truth-charged statement: "And the angel answered and said to her, "The Holy Spirit will come *upon* you, and the **power** (*dunamis*, Gr.) of the Most High will *overshadow* you; and, *for* **that** *reason*"—the reason that the *Holy Spirit has come* **upon** *her*, and that *the* **power** *of the Most High has* **overshadowed** *her*, for **that** reason—"the holy offspring shall be called *the Son of God*." It is so important that you retain that thought—that it is for **that** reason that He shall be called the Son of God, because we shall see that point being further established later.

"And Mary said, "Behold, the bondslave of the Lord; **be it done unto me according to your word**." Now friend, if you want to know the precise moment Jesus was conceived in the womb of Mary, *that* is the point, *that* is the juncture, right there—when she said (despite her not being able to comprehend *how* this could be, she did not *disbelieve* it), "Behold, the bondslave of the Lord"—she was saying, I am your bondslave, Lord, whatever you want—"be it done unto me according to your word"—*at that very moment*, Jesus was conceived in her womb by virtue of her receiving the implantation of the Seed of God into an unfertilized human egg.

Now, friends, it is the same way when we are born again: we say, "Be it done to me according to your Word." The "Word" is Jesus—the Word that was made flesh and became the Incarnate Son of God, Jesus (John 1:1-14; 1 Jn. 1:1-3). And when we accept the Living and Abiding Word of God in our hearts, the Bible says, we are at that moment born again, regenerated, spiritually revived by the Spirit.

We accept Him into our *heart*—Mary accepted what the angel of the Lord said, a message, or *word*, from God in her heart, and at that moment the *Sperma* of God, which means the *Seed* of God in the Greek, was implanted and the Word made Flesh was conceived in her *womb*. It is in like manner that each of us is born again—by accepting, receiving the Seed of God, the Word of God, Jesus, into our *spiritual womb*—our *heart*, or *human spirit* (cf., Jas. 1:21).

And so, again, we find in all this that it was not necessary for Jesus to be born again in the way humans must be born again, because Jesus was the Seed of God, the Son of God, God the Son, who was born of the Holy Spirit. He was *begotten* from God. He was not *born* from the human lineage that was contaminated with the sin nature going back to Adam. But it was necessary that Jesus first be "born" or birthed into humanity as a *human*, taking on a human body, human form, in order that He could become the Incarnate Son of God who the angel spoke about.

Later, we'll also see the precise moment when Jesus became the Beloved Son of God in whom God the Father was well-pleased.

Chapter Three
Jesus—The Baptizer in the Holy Spirit

Now the second point that is vital to our discussion, and vital to unraveling all of the distortion and confusion regarding this crucial matter of the Baptism in the Holy Spirit, is that Jesus Himself, who is our Model, was the *Prototype* of the Sons of God. He is our *spiritual model* in all spiritual things, and as such, Jesus Himself was *baptized* in the Holy Spirit, and thereby became the *Baptizer* in the Holy Spirit. He Himself was baptized in the Holy Spirit, and it was through that experience of being baptized Himself in the Holy Spirit that He became the Baptizer in the Holy Spirit. Well, you see, you cannot *give* something that you have not *received*. And Jesus first *received* the Baptism in the Holy Spirit *Himself*, and was empowered with the Holy Spirit. It is vital for us to understand that about the Baptism in the Holy Spirit.

In fact, one of the things that the Church often fails to recognize is that everything that Jesus did here on Earth, He did not do as *God*. Indeed, the Bible tells us in Philippians (2:6-8) that before coming down to the Earth and being born of the Virgin Mary, being conceived in her womb and delivered, being given birth to, before that, He divested Himself of, laid aside, His deity, in order to come to Earth and be born as a Man, a Human. Indeed, it was required that He lay aside, or cast off as removing a garment, the original language indicates, His deity to allow Him to be able to be born as a Human. So, what He did here on the Earth during His fleshly ministry, it is vital to understand, He did not do as *God*; but rather as a *Man* baptized in the Holy Ghost.

Jesus stated that the works that He did, shall we, believers, do also, and even greater works shall we do. But, it is virtually impossible to do, not only the works Jesus did but even greater works than what He did, without being baptized in the Holy Ghost, in the same manner as Jesus Himself was baptized in the Holy Ghost. As I said, Jesus is our Model in all spiritual things, and He set the precedent that in order to be a believer, i.e., a son of God who is well-pleasing to God, and who is doing the works of God, you must be baptized in the Holy Ghost. How anyone believes that he or she can be a disciple of Jesus—a follower of Jesus, a learner of Jesus—without following His example of being baptized in the Holy Ghost is entirely beyond my understanding.

So we're going to examine just two Scriptures here demonstrating that Jesus Himself was baptized in Holy Spirit and thereby became the Baptizer in the Holy Spirit. The first of those texts is Luke 3:16-23, which reads, "John (the Baptist), answered and said to them all, 'As for me, I baptize you with *water.*'" In Matthew's version of what John stated, recorded in Matthew 3:11, John says that he baptized "in *water* <u>for repentance</u>, but He who is coming after me is mightier than I, and I am not even fit to remove His sandals; *He Himself* (i.e., Jesus) will baptize you with <u>the Holy Spirit</u> and with <u>fire</u>."

And Bible scholars and historians agree that nowhere in recorded history is there any evidence that Jesus Himself ever baptized *anyone* in water. You see, the baptism in water for repentance is a baptism that is conducted by *men* as a testimony of repentance, but the baptism in the Holy Ghost, the Baptism in the Holy Spirit and Fire, is a baptism that *Jesus Himself* performs. *Jesus is the Baptizer in the Holy Spirit— the Living Waters of God!* His baptism is for supernatural empowerment, not repentance! Repentance is *our* part. Empowerment is *Jesus'* part.

> Now it came about when all the people were baptized *(this is talking about being baptized in water),* that Jesus also was baptized, and while He was praying, heaven was opened, and the Holy Spirit descended upon Him in bodily form like a dove, and a voice came out of heaven, 'Thou art My beloved Son, **in Thee I am well-pleased.**" (Lk. 3:21-22)

Now I want you to notice several things about this passage. Number one, it says, that "heaven was opened up." Now, Friends, have you ever needed Heaven to be opened up in your life, in order that you might receive something from God? Have you ever needed the Heavens to be opened that you might receive enablement and empowerment from God? Well, that is what happens when you follow in the pattern that Jesus set of receiving the Baptism in the Holy Spirit. I'll talk more about that as we progress.

Then, in verse twenty-two, notice it says, "And the Holy Spirit descended upon Him." And, as I pointed out so conclusively previously, Jesus was originally born of the Holy Spirit, and so, because of that, He always had the Holy Spirit in Him, thus He did not have to be born again as unredeemed humans who are all born with the sin nature permeating them do, but rather He was born with the Holy Spirit permeating Him already. And so, regardless of diverse teachings you may have heard in this regard, this experience here that took place was not an experience in which Jesus was receiving the Holy Spirit *inside* of Him. Rather, it clearly says that the Holy Spirit descended *upon* Him in bodily form, like a Dove. So, the Holy Spirit is not just ethereal; He has a spiritual body, and He can come in a *form*—in this case, He came in the *form* of a *Dove* as a sign that John would see. Perhaps others saw this event as well, but we *know* that John the Baptist saw it, because Scripture says he did. And, he saw it as a sign that this was the Messiah, the Christ, the Son of God.

We need to take note of what the Holy Spirit is pointing out here in this writing in Luke, Chapter 3, verse 21. It says at that moment—when He was baptized by John and was praying—the Holy Spirit descended upon Jesus in bodily form, the form of a Dove. Now, never before in Jesus' life did this occur; but this occurred at this moment—"a voice came out of heaven." Now, no matter who you are, and what your background is, certainly you can agree with me: this is an unprecedented and extraordinary event, and we need to take note of what precipitated it—it was that the

Holy Spirit descended upon Jesus in the form of a Dove, and that the voice of God said, "Thou art My Beloved *Son*, in Thee I am **well-pleased**."

Jesus was the *Prototype* of **all** the Sons of God—the Bible says so. When it says, the "firstborn" in various passages (Lk. 2:7,23; Rom. 8:29; Col. 1:15,18; Heb. 1:6; 11:28; 12:23; Rev. 1:5) it is talking about literally, the *prototype*—the Greek word in those passages means *prototype*. Jesus is the *Prototype* of all of the Sons of God. And, when Jesus received the Baptism in the Holy Ghost, God said at that moment, "Thou art My Beloved *Son*, in Thee I am well-pleased."

Now let me ask you: Do you want to be well-pleasing to God? Well, you can be! It's simple, you must follow the pattern that Jesus set. If this was the pattern that Jesus had to follow in order to be well-pleasing to God, then certainly it is not difficult to understand that if you and I want to be pleasing to God, we must also follow that same pattern—to receive the Baptism in the Holy Ghost.

And, then, there's an absolutely vital principle that is indicated in verse 23, which says, "And when He began His ministry, Jesus Himself was about thirty years of age." A vital principle that is often overlooked by intellectual Christianity is that Jesus did not begin His ministry until after that the Holy Ghost had descended upon Him, until after that He received the Baptism in the Holy Ghost. Do you understand that? What makes anybody think that they can begin *their* ministry—a ministry that is supposed to be *of* the Spirit, *by* the Spirit, *through* the Spirit, and the Spirit operating through *them*—without receiving the Baptism in the Holy Spirit, is totally beyond my ability to comprehend.

Continuing with establishing the point that Jesus Himself was baptized in the Holy Spirit, and thereby became the Baptizer in the Holy Spirit, let's look at another passage of Scripture, which is Acts 2:33. This passage of Scripture comes on the backdrop of what happened on the Day of Pentecost, which was that the Holy Ghost came in the form of a mighty rushing wind, filled the whole house where the

Jesus — The Baptizer in the Holy Spirit

disciples were, and "there appeared unto them," it says in verses three and four of Acts, Chapter 2:

> There appeared unto them tongues as of fire distributing themselves and they rested on each one of them and they were all filled with the Holy Spirit and began to speak with other tongues as the spirit was giving them utterance.

And when the devout Jews who had traveled from all over the world to Jerusalem for the Feast of Pentecost heard them speaking in the various native tongues of the regions and nations they were from, some began mocking and accusing them of being inebriated from new wine at this early time in the morning. And the Apostle Peter then, after some considerable time had passed—we don't know how long—but he eventually "stood up," the account says—probably he stood up because he wasn't standing up previously, probably because he *couldn't* stand up, because probably when the Holy Ghost came upon these people, I have no doubt that many, if not all of them, were slain in the Spirit, or were unable to stand under the manifest power of this outpouring of the Spirit. And so the Apostle Peter, rising to his feet, he began to preach—with new anointing! Three-thousand were saved that day as a result of his anointed message!

But, in verse 33, Luke records that Peter says something particularly powerful and profound. In fact, let's read into it beginning in verse 32: "This Jesus, God raised up again, to which we are all *witnesses*." And that's what the power of the Holy Ghost is all about! Jesus said that, "You shall receive *power* to be My *witnesses*." And, this power that was poured out on the Day of Pentecost—*Dunamis-Power*—is supernatural empowerment of the Spirit to be *witnesses* of the Resurrection of the Lord Jesus Christ, that He is alive, that He lives yet today, that His power is on-going, that He did not die, death and the grave could not hold Him, but He was raised from the dead!

Then, in verse 33, Peter said, "Therefore, having been exalted to the right hand of God and having received from the Father the promise of the Holy Spirit, He has poured forth (He, Jesus, has poured forth) this which you both see and hear." Now, please understand, it is saying that it is *Jesus* Who is the One that poured this forth! Remember that John the Baptist, the original Baptist said, "As for me, I baptize you with water for repentance, but He who is coming after me is mightier than I...*He will baptize you with the Holy Spirit and fire*" (Mat. 3:11), and that is exactly what occurred on the Day of Pentecost!

Notice also the fact that it says here in this verse, "Therefore having been highly exalted to the right hand of God, and having *received* from the Father, the promise of the Holy Spirit." One cannot *give* something that he has not first *received*. Jesus *received* the Holy Spirit, as we have seen previously—we have seen that Jesus was Himself baptized in the Holy Ghost, and *that* therefore gave Him the authority and capability to baptize others in the Holy Ghost.

And, it was Jesus Himself, Peter said, who had "poured out" this Dunamis-Power *after* He had ascended on high and *after* He had sat down at the right hand of God. This outpouring then was a work of Jesus; it was a part of Jesus, for He is the Baptizer in the Holy Spirit! How then could the Baptism in the Holy Spirit not be of God, or be of the devil, or not be something God wants for His people, as many have been taught and believe, if it is the work of Jesus, something that *He* did? To purport such is absolutely ludicrous, but worse than that, it is *blasphemous*! Jesus and the Holy Spirit are inextricably linked or connected. They are both Members of the Godhead! If we want to receive *all* of Jesus, all of God, we must receive what He is pouring out, and He is pouring out the Living Water of the Spirit via the Baptism in the Holy Ghost. He not only did it over 2,000 years ago on the Day of Pentecost, but He is still doing it today! "Jesus Christ is the same yesterday and today and forever" (Heb. 13:8)! That same Dunamis-Power is still available to *anyone* today who would but ask for and receive it through the Baptism in the Holy Spirit! To refuse the Baptism in the Holy Spirit is to refuse God, and is utter blasphemy!

Now another point that is absolutely vital to extract from this passage is what Peter said, "Having received from the Father the promise of the Holy Spirit." Many Bible expositors try to teach that the Baptism in the Holy Spirit and the work of the Holy Spirit in regeneration are the same thing, or that they occur at the same time, or other variations of that hypothesis. And, they will put their own humanly-invented spin on Acts 1:4, where it says, "And gathering them together, Jesus commanded them not to leave Jerusalem but to wait for what the Father had promised." And, they will say that what it was that the Father had promised was the Holy Spirit in salvation; that salvation is "the promise of the Father." Now, my friends, I hate to be so direct, but I must say that that is the most ludicrous and absurd theology, not to mention faulty Bible scholarship, that I have ever heard! And, that becomes clear just by reading this First Chapter of the Book of Acts, where the writer, Luke, says:

> The first account I composed, Theophilus, about all that Jesus began to do and teach, until the day when He was taken up, after He had by the Holy Spirit given orders to the apostles whom He had chosen.

And in his "first account" that he is talking about, which is the Gospel of Luke, he says in Chapter 24, beginning in verse 45,

> Then He opened their minds to understand the Scriptures, and He said to them, "Thus it is written, that the Christ should suffer and rise again from the dead the third day; and that repentance for forgiveness of sin should be proclaimed in His name to all the nations, beginning from Jerusalem. You are witnesses of these things. And, behold, I am sending forth the promise of My Father upon you; but you are to stay in the city until you are clothed with power from on high."

Now, as Luke said in the Book of Acts, this is talking about right before Jesus ascended on high. Prior to that, when they were in the Upper Room, is when the apostles and the other disciples were born again. They were infused or filled with the Holy Spirit, receiving the regenerative work of the Holy Spirit in salvation, not on the Day of Pentecost, but on the *evening* of Resurrection Sunday, which many refer to by the pagan assignation of "Easter Sunday."

Churches and Christians make such a to-do of celebrating the Resurrection *morning*—on what most of them call *Easter*—when some of the disciples went to the tomb and found the tomb was empty, just as Jesus prophesied it would be—that few recognize or even know what happened subsequently that day and evening, which is even more significant and miraculous. Outside the empty tomb when Mary finally recognized the person talking to her who she had presumed to be the caretaker of the tomb was actually Jesus, she attempted to embrace Him, but Jesus said to her, "Mary, touch Me not, *for I am not yet ascended unto My Father*" (Jn. 20:17). He would not allow her to touch Him because He was now the True High Priest all the thousands of years of surrogate Hebrew high priests typified, who would momentarily on that Resurrection Sunday ascend into Heaven to present Himself to God as the Ransom for our redemption. He was both the spotless sacrificial Lamb of God whose substitutionary death takes away the sins of the world **and** the true High Priest who would offer up Himself as the guiltless redemption Ransom that must be paid to purchase pardon for the guilty. In Zechariah 3, is described that glorious exchange that transpired that day when the resurrected Christ ascended and was received into Heaven by God. But, being touched by a woman during this time of consecration as the High Priest prior to His ascension would have defiled and disqualified Him as the High Priest, and negated the gloriously splendiferous transactions that would transpire when He presented Himself before the Almighty God and Supreme Judge!

But, on that Resurrection Evening, the Bible says the apostles and 108 other disciples were in the Upper Room, having shut and locked the doors, for fear of the Jews, and suddenly the resurrected Jesus, in His resurrected Body came right through those locked doors and appeared to all those present. Praise God! Aren't you glad that Jesus will not allow the doors that we've locked to keep Him out of our lives actually keep Him out of our lives? Hallelujah!

Jesus burst through those locked doors and appeared unto the 120 disciples present, declaring "Shalom!"—because He had now established peace between God and Man—and showing them "by many convincing proofs" (Ac. 1:3) that it was indeed He! Do you understand what this story is saying? It is saying that the first word out of Jesus' mouth when He returned to Earth after having offered Himself to God as the Ransom for our redemption was "Peace!"—because He was declaring that all was now well, peace had been established, the enmity had been removed, between God and Man! God's righteous and just wrath against wicked sinners—you and me and every person ever born except Jesus—had now been appeased, once and for all!

Finally, then, He breathed upon them, and said, "Receive, ye the Holy Spirit!" (Jn. 20:22). It was at that moment that these first disciples received the Holy Spirit in regeneration for the first time, as Jesus infused it into them. At that moment, they became the very first group of people who were ever born again in human history! Think of that! Marvel at that! It is truly marvelous and mindboggling!

No one *could* have been born again *before* Christ's substitutionary death on the Cross as the Lamb of God, or *before* He descended into Hell and rose triumphantly having conquered death, Hell, and the grave on the third day, or *before* He ascended into Heaven to present Himself as the True High Priest offering up Himself as a Ransom for the sins and offenses of all humanity. But, when He had accomplished all that in three days, He came back in His resurrected Spiritual Body, announced Shalom! and breathed on the 120 disciples, and said, "Receive ye the Holy Spirit!" At that moment these disciples—*all of them*—were instantaneously *born again* and received the *regenerative* working of the Holy Spirit.

But, it was *after* all this transpired that Jesus was saying to the apostles and the other disciples, "I am sending forth *the promise of the Father **upon** you*. But you are to stay in the city until you are *clothed with power* from on high" (Lk. 24:49). He obviously was talking about a *different* "promise of the Father," not the promise of *salvation*, but rather the promise of what happened later, on the Day of Pentecost. We know that because in the Book of Acts, the writer, Luke, records Jesus' words to the disciples in response to their question regarding whether or not what He was talking about was the prophesied time that the Messiah would restore "the kingdom to Israel":

> "It is not for you to know the times or epochs which the Father has fixed by his own authority; *but you shall receive power when the Holy Spirit has come upon you*; and you shall be My witnesses both in Jerusalem and in Judea and Samaria, and even the remotest parts of the earth." (Ac. 1:7-8)

Then followed all the things that took place that day that I delineated. Then, we go again to Acts 2:33, where we read again Peter's exuberant assertion, "Therefore, having been exalted to the right hand of God, and having received from the Father the promise (as I established already, the Father's promise was the *Baptism in the Holy Spirit*), He has *poured forth* this which you both *see and hear*."

Friend, when you truly receive the true Baptism in the Holy Ghost, there's no way you can keep it quiet or keep people from seeing and hearing it! You *will* be filled to overflowing with "power from on high," and other people *will* hear it, and other people *will* see it—as they observe all the miraculous things that begin happening in your life! They will hear and see what's happened in your life, for your life shall be significantly and substantively changed because it is now charged with a dimension of divine power that was not there before, for now you have been imbued with *power from on high*!

Chapter Four
The Spirit's Work in Regeneration

Now the truth that I am going to establish from Scripture in this segment concerns the first work of the Holy Spirit in regeneration, that is, in the born-again experience, or salvation, so that we can contrast that working of the Holy Spirit against the working of the Holy Spirit in the Baptism in the Holy Spirit—demonstrating that these are two separate and distinct experiences for the believer and workings of the Holy Spirit.

You Must Be Born Again

The first passage of Scripture we want to look at is in John 3:3-8. Jesus is explaining to a Pharisee named Nicodemus, who, we are told, was a "ruler of the Jews," the requisite of being born again:

> Jesus answered and said to him, "Truly, truly, I say to you, unless one is born again, he cannot see the kingdom of God." Nicodemus said to him, "How can a man be born when he is old. He cannot enter a second time into his mother's womb and be born, can he?" Jesus answered, "Truly, truly, I say to you, unless one is born of water and the Spirit, he cannot enter into the kingdom of God. That which is born of the flesh is flesh, and that which is born of the Spirit is spirit. Do not be amazed that I said to you, 'You must be born again.' The wind blows where it wishes and you hear the sound of it, but do not know where it comes from and where it is going; so is everyone who is born of the Spirit."

Now, clearly, in this passage, Jesus, is talking about being *born* by the Spirit of God. He is referring to the initial transaction of *regeneration*, when Jesus comes in the form of the Holy Spirit to live—i.e , reside or abide—in a person's spiritual heart, which is the human spirit, at the very moment when he/she asks Jesus for forgiveness of their previous sins and that He come and live in his/her heart and life.

Now, in Ephesians 2:1, it explains to us that we *were* dead in our trespasses and sins. You recall that in the Garden of Eden, when God spoke to Adam and Eve and told them not to eat of the tree of the knowledge of good and evil, for He said that in the day that they ate of it, they would surely die. Yet, we see that they lived for over 900 years, after they disobeyed God's explicit commandment and ate anyway. Well, what, then, was God referring to when He said they would die? They *did* indeed die when they partook of the fruit of the tree of the knowledge of good and evil, which was the *carnal nature,* the *sin nature,* but it was not *physical* death that transpired, but rather *spiritual* death, in that their human spirit died. That is what produced the result the Apostle Paul was speaking about in his epistle to the Ephesians:

> And you were dead in your trespasses and sins, in which you formerly walked according to the course of this world, according to the prince of the power of the air, of the spirit that is now working in the sons of disobedience. (Eph. 2:1-2)

As I said, and this is a critical matter to understand, the fruit of the tree of the knowledge of good and evil of which Adam and Eve partook was not an apple as the mythology of the Creation purports, but rather it was the carnal or sin nature, "the spirit that is now working in the sons of disobedience," which is "according to the course of this world, according to the prince of the power of the air,"—who is Satan. Satan is the "prince of the power of the air." It is his spirit—"the spirit that is now working in the sons of disobedience" that permeates and pervades the atmosphere on Earth, which is the prime cause of all evil and wickedness upon the Earth.

Alive But Dead

So, how is it that humans can be alive and living, but yet dead at the same time? That's a very good and important question, the answer to which is fundamental to the Gospel. The Bible makes it clear that humans are tripartite beings, that is, consisting of three parts. As God is Triune, consisting of *three* Persons—Father, Son, and Holy Spirit—yet being *one* Divinity, or Godhead, so also we, having been made in the Image of God (Gen. 1:26,27), were made in three parts—spirit, soul, and body (1 Thes. 5:23)—and thus are tripartite beings. We **are** essentially a *spirit*. God is Spirit (Jn. 4:24), and being made by Him and in His image, we are also essentially *spirit*. Moreover, in the original Creation, God also formed Man a physical body out of the dirt of the ground and breathed or infused the "breath of Life," i.e., God's very Breath or Spirit (both the Hebrew and Greek word for *spirit* is the same word for *breath*), and Man thereby became a "living soul": "And the LORD God formed man of the dust of the ground, and breathed into his nostrils the breath of life; and man became a living soul" (Gen. 2:7).

So, the result is that humans are first and foremost a *spirit*, who **have** a *soul*, which is made up of our mind, will and emotions, and, then the spirit and soul is contained or enshrouded **in** a physical human *body*. So, we have three parts, and are tripartite beings.

But, in the Garden of Eden, when Adam and Eve sinned against God by partaking of the fruit of the tree of the knowledge of good and evil, in direct disobedience to God's explicit commandment not to, their human spirit died. Moreover, everyone who has ever been born, every human being that has ever been born since then, has been born with a human spirit that exists, but is *dead* spiritually. It is spiritually dead. That is what Ephesians 2:1 is speaking about when it says, "And you were *dead* in your trespasses and sins." The entire progeny of Adam and Eve—all humanity—are born into this world spiritually *dead. That* is the reason we all "must be born again."

Spiritual Resurrection

When Jesus comes to live in our spiritually dead human spirit, it becomes *alive*, as it is infused with the *regenerative* power of the Holy Spirit. By that infusion of the Spirit into our dead human spirit we are literally raised from the dead, resurrected, just as Jesus was raised from the dead or resurrected, only spiritually rather than physically (cf., Rom. 8:10-11).

That—what I was just talking about—is the *initial* working of the Holy Spirit in our lives—what takes place when we are born again. But, again, that is the *regenerative* working of the Holy Spirit, when the Holy Spirit comes to live in our spiritual hearts or human spirits. When we ask Jesus to come and live in our hearts, He *regenerates* our human spirit. He gives *Life* to our spirit at that moment of the rebirth. But that experience and working of the Holy Spirit in *regeneration*, or the new birth, is separate and distinct from the working of the Holy Spirit that takes place through the *Baptism* in the Holy Spirit.

In verse six of the text cited at the beginning of this chapter, Jesus said, "That which is born of the flesh is flesh," referring to the natural birth. Then, He said, "and that which is born of the Spirit is spirit." And, what He was describing there is when we are born again, when Jesus comes to live in our spirit, our human spirit, in the form of the Holy Spirit, it is at that moment that the *regenerative* working of the Holy Spirit begins to *regenerate* our human spirit, which *was* dead in our trespasses and sins, according to Ephesians 2:1, as a result of the spiritual death that took place when Adam and Eve fell into perdition in the Garden of Eden.

A Well of Water Springing Up Unto Eternal Life

Now, in the story regarding the woman of Samaria, who met Jesus as she came to Jacob's Well to draw water, Jesus made an allegorical reference to what transpires at this moment of regeneration when someone gives his or her life to Jesus, and He comes in the form of the Holy Spirit to regenerate that person's human spirit, infusing them with spiritual life. It is the Life of God by which we are infused in the form of the Holy Spirit taking up residence in our human spirit at the point of salvation, when Jesus comes to live within our heart. And it is very important to give great attention to the details of what Jesus was saying in this story and what He is revealing to us regarding the Holy Spirit.

The story is recounted in John 4:7-14: "There came a woman of Samaria to draw water. Jesus said to her, "Give Me **a drink**." Now notice He is referring to **"a drink,"** and that is very important, and I will explain the significance of that as we continue on.

> "Therefore, the Samaritan woman said to Him, "How is it that You, being a Jew ask me for **a drink**, since I am a Samaritan woman? (For Jews have no dealings with the Samaritans.)" Notice again, the issue is: **"a drink."**

The account continues, "Jesus answered and said to her, 'If you knew the **gift of God**.'" Notice, what He refers to this "drink" as—He calls it, "the **gift of God**"—this "drink" that He is referring to here. Picking the text back up, Jesus said:

> "If you knew the gift of God and who it is who says to you, 'Give Me **a drink**,' you would have asked Him and He would have given you living water." She said to Him, "Sir, You have nothing to draw with and the well is deep, where then do You get that living water? You are not greater than our father Jacob, are You, who gave us the well and drank of it himself and his sons and his cattle?" Jesus answered and said to her, "Everyone who drinks of this water *(the water that is in the well that you are referring to, the physical water)* will thirst again; but whoever **drinks of the water that I will give him** shall never thirst; but the water that I will give him will become in him **a well of water *springing up* to ETERNAL LIFE**." *[Parenthetical explanation and emphases added]*

Now that's such a critical thing that Jesus said there. He referred to this water as being a *well*, He said it "will become in him **a well of water**"—"a well of water springing up to eternal life." A *well* of water is something that *contains* water, it *holds* the water, it is an enclosed *container* of the water, a vessel in which the water is enclosed. And He said that this "well of water" would *spring up* to **Eternal Life**. So, the issue that He is speaking about here in this conversation with this woman at Jacob's Well is the issue of the Living Waters of the Holy Spirit in **Eternal Life**.

Hence, what Jesus is describing here is the work of the Holy Spirit in *regeneration* or *spiritual rebirth*, or the moment of salvation, in which we are "…saved…by the washing of *regeneration* and *renewing* by the Holy Spirit" (Tit. 3:5). This working of the Holy Spirit can also be referred to as the *infusion* of the Holy Spirit.

But, as we shall see next, there is another or adjunct working of the Holy Spirit in the life of the regenerated, or Born Again, believer, which is the work of the Holy Spirit in the *Baptism or Immersion* in the Holy Spirit.

Chapter Five
The Spirit's Work in Spirit-Baptism

Now the truth I am going to establish from Scripture in this chapter is that the Baptism in the Holy Spirit is another or adjunct work of the Holy Spirit that is separate and distinct from the working of the Holy Spirit in *regeneration*, i.e., spiritual *rebirth* or *salvation*. To begin that explanation, I want to turn first to John 7:37-39. Here it says:

> Now on the last day, the great day of the feast, Jesus stood and cried out, saying, "If anyone is thirsty, let him come to Me and drink. He who believes in Me, as the Scripture said, 'From his innermost being will flow *rivers of living water*.'" But this He spoke of **the Spirit, whom those who believed in Him were to receive**; for the Spirit was not yet given, because Jesus was not yet glorified.

Rivers of Living Water

Now, you recall in the previous chapter we talked about the story of the woman at the well. And Jesus spoke what He spoke at Jacob's Well because He was talking about the working of the Holy Spirit—the Living Water—in rebirth or regeneration or salvation. To do so, He invoked an analogy comparing the natural water in Jacob's Well, which could only quench physical thirst, to the Living Water's work in regeneration when the Holy Spirit comes into a person and regenerates or renews their spiritually dead human spirit, becoming "a *well* of water, springing up to *eternal life*."

But notice the difference of what Jesus was speaking about here "on the last day, the great day of the Feast" of Booths or Tabernacles, in the passage quoted previously, John, Chapter 7, verses 37 through 39. In verse 38, He said,

"He who believes in Me, as the Scriptures said, from his innermost being will *flow*...." Now a *well* does not have a *flow* of water. In fact, people have to dip into it in order to draw water out of it, as Jesus was asking that Samaritan woman to do: "Give Me a drink." She would have had to dip into the well with a bucket, or some container she had brought with her to the well, to bring out water from it. A well is not something out of which the water *flows* on its own; it is a *container* of water; it contains the water. But, Jesus speaks here of *rivers* of living water. He said, "From his **innermost being** will *flow* rivers of living water." In fact, Jesus speaks not of *a* river—singular—but *rivers*—plural—of Living Water. As we shall see, that is an important distinction. Moreover, it also distinguishes the analogy of "rivers of living water" from "a well of water" Jesus invoked in the previous analogy of Jacob's Well in His conversation with the Samaritan woman at Jacob's Well.

Notice also that He identified the well from which these rivers of living water flow as the born again believer's "innermost being," which is a term referring to the human spirit. The King James translators rendered the Greek word Jesus invoked *koilia* as "belly," but it was a figurative connotation Jesus was evoking referring to what the NASB translators more appropriately for modern English usage rendered "innermost being," which is a reference to the human spirit. Every human being has a human spirit, albeit at birth it is "dead in your trespasses and sins" (Eph. 2:1), which means we are born into spiritual death, or in other words, when we are born physically we are dead spiritually. That human spirit with which we are all born, which is a spiritual and non-physical specter, if you will, or of the spirit realm vis-à-vis physical, is located somewhere behind the stomach in the human anatomy. This is why Jesus called it the "innermost being." I realize such matters are subject to mockery and ridicule by intellectual agnosticism, but that detracts not one iota from the truth of it. Though I will say that human language sometimes fails when attempting to describe spiritual matters, which, as the

Apostle Paul explained, are "spiritually appraised": "But a natural man does not accept the things of the Spirit of God, *for they are foolishness to him;* and he cannot understand them, **because they are spiritually appraised**" (1 Cor. 2:14). Spiritual things can only be understood through the Spirit; the intellect cannot understand them.

Now, in this dissertation in John 7:37-39 we are examining, Jesus is talking about something that is going to **flow out**, not something that is merely being **contained** in, as He was speaking about in regeneration, when our human spirit becomes the spiritual "well" that contains the Holy Spirit, and that Living Water of the Holy Spirit contained in our human spirit *springs up* to **Eternal Life**. Here, in this monologue, He's talking about something that's *flowing out* of people like a river—a river of endless flow of Living Water. And how true this is—in regeneration the Holy Spirit comes to that person who has been regenerated by the Spirit, bringing with Him the Zoe-Life of God. Inherent in the *Life* of God is the *Nature* of God—"the Divine Nature" of which Peter declared Born Again believers are partakers (2 Pet. 1:4). "The Divine Nature is God's Life (*Zoe*, Gr.), and with the Divine Nature comes the *attributes* of God, what Scripture calls "the *fruit* of the Spirit," which are identified specifically in Galatians 5:22-23:

> But the fruit of the Spirit is love, joy, peace, patience, kindness, goodness, faithfulness, gentleness, self-control; against such things there is no law. (Gal. 5:22-23)

It is at that time that the believer receives the *Life of God* that he/she receives into his/her now regenerated human spirit the *fruit* of the Spirit, which is an inherent part of the Divine Nature or Life of God. Again, human words or language sometimes are inadequate and fail when attempting to describe spiritual matters, but what I am trying to point out is that with the infusion of the Life of God by the agency of the Holy Spirit, who is the Divine Nature, which consists of the attributes of God—i.e., "the fruit of the Spirit," these fruit/attributes are injected into the regenerated human spirit. Again, the attributes of God inherent in the Divine Nature, are what the Apostle Paul delineated as "the fruit of the Spirit."

Now, it is vital to understand that I am *not* saying that believers, having been infused with the Life of God, or the Divine Nature, are then themselves "divine" or deity, as some critics erroneously allege it is being said, implicitly or explicitly in teaching on this matter. I will state categorically that believers do *not* then become divine or deity at the new birth, because it is only their *spirit* in which regeneration occurs and is born again, but the carnal nature, the sin nature, "the spirit now working in the sons of disobedience" still abides in their unperfected, unsaved, unrevived *soul* and *body*, which condition will not change until the sounding of "the last trump of God," when "in a moment, in the twinkling of an eye, at the last trumpet; for the trumpet will sound…and **we will be changed**" (1 Cor. 15:52). It is at that glorious moment—when all believers receive "the redemption of our body" (Rom. 8:23)—that the sin nature shall be removed or eradicated from the redeemed!

That transaction of rebirth or regeneration, resulting from the infusion of the human spirit with or by the Holy Spirit, though others will certainly benefit from the resultant transformation in the heart and life of the regenerated believer, is preeminently for **that** person who has experienced regeneration and **their** *rightstanding* with God, **their** *relationship* with God. That's the import of the portion of Jesus' statement: "*springing up* to **eternal life**." He is describing an upward-downward, vertical, coursing of the Living Water of the Holy Spirit, from a filled human spirit to God, establishing, or more accurately, reestablishing, the relationship of the person receiving the Holy Spirit with God through the *infusion* of the Holy Spirit.

But, in the second working of the Holy Spirit, it is "*rivers* of living water," that begin to *flow **out*** of the person's human spirit who has been baptized, or immersed, in the Spirit. And, what is imparted at that point is the *gifts* of the Spirit, because the gifts of the Spirit (*charismata*, Gr.) are supernatural gifts that are given by the Holy Spirit, the pre-eminent and primary object and beneficiary of which is *other* people rather than that person who is baptized or immersed. Chapter Twelve is devoted to discussing those gifts of the Spirit.

And so, again, we see that Jesus Himself is making a distinction between the *baptism* or *immersion* in the Holy Spirit and what happens in regeneration with the *infusion* of the Holy Spirit when the Holy Spirit comes to take up residence in the human heart or spirit.

Again, to state it succinctly, in regeneration the Holy Spirit comes to live *in* the believer, bringing the Life of God, manifest in the form of the **fruit** of the Spirit, making the believer a *container* of the Life of God, and establishing his/her relationship with God. In the Spirit-Baptism, the Holy Spirit comes *upon* or *on* the believer, bestowing the **power** of God, manifest in the *gifts* of the Spirit, making the believer a *conduit*, contrasted to a *container*—a *conduit* through which the supernatural gifting of the Holy Spirit *flows **out*** of the believer unto others, as opposed to being *resident **in*** the believer.

The Promise of the Father

Now, in previous sections, we established the fact that, as recorded in John 20:22, the early disciples, including the apostles, received the working of the Holy Spirit in regeneration on Resurrection Evening, when Jesus came through the locked door and appeared before the disciples. In this section, we want to look more closely at what Jesus called, "the promise of the Father" to demonstrate further that He was not referring to the working of the Holy Spirit in regeneration or salvation. And, to do that we will be reemphasizing some of the points we have already established. Picking up the text in verse 19 of John, Chapter 20, it says:

> When therefore it was evening, on that day, the first day of the week, and when the doors were shut, where the disciples were, for fear of the Jews, Jesus came and stood in their midst, and said to them, "Peace be with you." And

when He had said this, He showed them both His hands and His side. The disciples therefore rejoiced when they saw the Lord. Jesus said to them again, "Peace be with you; as the Father has sent Me, I also send you." And when He had said this, He breathed on them, and said to them, "**Receive the Holy Spirit**."

Now, in simple terms, when Jesus breathed upon the disciples, He was for the first time dispensing the Holy Spirit for regeneration unto them, that is, to be saved. It was at that moment that the early disciples were saved. This was the first dispensing of the Holy Spirit in salvation after Jesus completed His mission as the High Priest in Heaven, thereby, providing salvation. It was at this point that the disciples were first saved, and experienced the New Birth, as a result of the regenerating work of the Holy Spirit.

But it was *after* that, over a period of forty days, that the Bible says that Jesus appeared unto the disciples. And it was at the close of those forty days that Jesus gathered the disciples together for one final time before ascending into Heaven to sit down on His Throne at the right hand of God. As recorded in Luke 24:44-49, He recounted to them the events that had taken place during His suffering, reminding them that the Scriptures prophesied that that was the way that the Christ would suffer, and that He had told them that He would rise again from the dead, the third day; and, that repentance for forgiveness of sins would be proclaimed in His name to all the nations, beginning from Jerusalem.

Then, Jesus said, in verse 48:

"You are witnesses of these things, and behold, I am sending forth the promise of My Father *upon* you, *(upon you, the promise of My Father, upon you)*; but you are to stay in the city until you are **clothed** with power from on high."

So, though the disciples were saved, and the Holy Spirit had come to live *within* them, still Jesus instructed the disciples to **wait** in Jerusalem until He sent forth yet another promise of God the Father *upon* them, which would result in them being clothed with power from on high, which is a reference to the **Baptism** in the Holy Spirit (cf., Ac. 1:8)

Now Luke, the writer of the Gospel of Luke, was also the author of the Book of Acts. And in his second book, Luke recounts again the last dissertation of Jesus prior to His ascension, in a text in Acts 1:1-8. However, he also adds some crucial details that did not appear in his synoptic book, the Gospel of Luke:

Act 1:1-8
(1) The first account I composed, Theophilus, about all that Jesus began to do and teach,
(2) until the day when He was taken up to heaven, after He had by the Holy Spirit given orders to the apostles whom He had chosen.
(3) To these He also presented Himself alive after His suffering, by many convincing proofs, appearing to them over a period of forty days and speaking of the things concerning the kingdom of God.
(4) Gathering them together, He commanded them not to leave Jerusalem, but to wait for what the Father had promised, "Which," He said, "you heard of from Me;
(5) for John baptized with water, but you will be baptized with the Holy Spirit not many days from now."
(6) So when they had come together, they were asking Him, saying, "Lord, is it at this time You are restoring the kingdom to Israel?"
(7) He said to them, "It is not for you to know times or epochs which the Father has fixed by His own authority;
(8) but you will receive power when the Holy Spirit has come upon you; and you shall be My witnesses both in Jerusalem, and in all Judea and Samaria, and even to the remotest part of the earth."

In verses four and five, he includes Jesus' interpretation of His phrase, "The promise of My Father," that He invoked in his first account, saying that they would be baptized in the Holy Spirit not many days from now. Jesus is here clearly and explicitly defining the promise of the Father as being the Baptism in the Holy Spirit, not *salvation*, as some anti-Spirit-Baptism teachers purport.

And then, in verse eight, Jesus explains that the effect of the Baptism in the Holy Spirit upon the disciples will be that they will receive supernatural *power—dunamis*, the Greek word is—to bear witness of Christ, in contrast to the *fruit* of the Spirit, imparted through the regenerative working of the Holy Spirit in the New Birth, that is, at the moment of salvation.

The Fulfillment of the Promise of the Father

Reviewing briefly, in the previous sections, we saw that the early disciples were born again by the working of the Holy Spirit in regeneration on Resurrection Evening, when Jesus came through the locked doors, appearing before them, and breathed upon them, and said, "Receive ye the Holy Spirit!" But, it was 40 days *after* that that Jesus gathered the disciples together, and told them to wait in Jerusalem until He sent forth yet another promise of God the Father *upon* them that would result in them being *clothed* with power from on high, which was a reference to the *Baptism* in the Holy Spirit, for now He was speaking about something coming *upon* them rather than *in* them, as the Holy Spirit had done on Resurrection Evening, when he breathed upon them, and said, "Receive ye the Holy Spirit." Obviously, clothing is worn on the outside, externally, not internally, again indicating this is speaking not about the *infusion* of the Spirit, but the *immersion* of the Spirit.

And, then, we also saw in Luke's second book, The Acts of the Apostles, that Jesus described this "promise of the Father" He invoked in the first account, by saying that they would "be baptized in the Holy Spirit not many days from now" (Acts 1:5). So, Jesus explicitly and clearly defined "the promise of the Father" as being the *Baptism* in the Holy Spirit, **not** the working of the Holy Spirit in *regeneration* at the New Birth.

But, as the saying goes, "The proof of the pudding is in the eating." And in Acts, Chapter 2, we see the proof of the pudding:

> When the day of Pentecost had come, they were all together in one place. And suddenly there came from Heaven a noise like a violent rushing wind, and it filled the whole house where they were sitting. And there appeared to them tongues as of fire distributing themselves, and they rested on each one of them. And they were all filled with the Holy Spirit and began to speak with other tongues, as the Spirit was giving them utterance. (Ac. 2:1-4)

This fulfillment of Jesus' prediction that occurred on the Day of Pentecost and is recorded in Acts 2, conclusively proved that the Baptism in the Holy Spirit with the accompanying evidence of the gifts of tongues is "the promise of the Father," and that it is a subsequent and separate experience to salvation. The disciples were saved in the Upper Room. There they had the fullness of the Holy Spirit infused into them. Yet, it was *after* salvation that they were *clothed with*, or enveloped *in*, or immersed *in*, which is the literal meaning of the word, "baptized," the Holy Spirit.

Even further evidence that that which occurred on the Day of Pentecost was the fulfillment of the prophesied "promise of the Father" is evident in Peter's declaration:

> But **this** is **that** which was spoken by the prophet Joel; And it shall come to pass in the last days, saith God, I will pour out of My Spirit upon all flesh: and your sons and your daughters shall prophesy, and your young men shall see visions, and your old men shall dream dreams: And on *My servants* and on *My handmaidens* I will pour out in those days of My Spirit; and they shall prophesy (Ac. 2:16-18; KJV).

The portion of Joel's prophecy reiterated by Peter, in verse 18 of Acts 2, "And on *My servants* and on *My handmaidens* I will pour out in those days of My Spirit; and they shall prophesy," offers further proof that this outpouring of the Spirit would fall upon *saved believers*, as a separate and subsequent experience to salvation.

The First Outpouring of the Spirit on the Day of Pentecost

Now, in this section, we are continuing to establish from Scripture the fact that the Baptism in the Holy Spirit that was poured out for the first time on the Day of Pentecost was a second experience for the early disciples, separate and distinct from what took place on Resurrection Sunday evening, when Jesus came into the locked room where they had gathered, and He appeared unto them and the first words that He said to them were, "Peace be unto you." For, He had established peace between God and man, and then He breathed upon them and said, "Receive ye the Holy Spirit." That moment was the first dispensing of the Holy Spirit in salvation after Jesus completed His priestly mission in Heaven, thereby providing salvation for the very first time. It was at this point that the disciples were saved and experienced the rebirth.

Again, I am going to prove conclusively from Scripture that that experience was separate and distinct from what took place on the Day of Pentecost, many days hence. In Luke 24, verses 44 through 49, it says, "Now He (Jesus) said to them, 'These are My words which I spoke to you while I was still with you, that all things which are written about Me in the Law of Moses and the prophets in the Psalms must be fulfilled." He was talking about what He had told them would take place during his period of suffering. And, it did indeed take place just as the Scripture had predicted and as He had told them it would.

Continuing on, it says:

Then He opened their minds to understand the Scriptures, and He said to them, "Thus it is written, that the Christ would suffer and rise again from the dead the third day, and that repentance for forgiveness of sins would be proclaimed in His name to all the nations, beginning from Jerusalem. You are witnesses of these things. And behold, I am sending forth *the promise of My Father* upon you; but you are to stay in the city until you are clothed with power from on high."

Now it is absolutely essential that as you read you see

The Spirit's Work in Spirit Baptism 43

that this entire event took place *after* Resurrection Sunday, *after* Jesus had appeared to them in the Upper Room and breathed upon them and said, "Receive ye the Holy Spirit." And, they received the Holy Spirit in regeneration and were saved for the very first time at that moment.

It was *after* that event that Jesus appeared to them and had this conversation with them. And, even though now they were already *born again* of the Spirit—they had already received the Holy Spirit in regeneration—now He told them to "wait for the promise of the Father," to wait in the city until they were *clothed with power* from on high.

Now notice the distinction there: He was not talking about receiving something on the *inside* of them as they had done when they received the Holy Spirit in regeneration on Resurrection Evening, but now He is talking about something that would come *upon* them, for He said, "I am sending forth the promise of the Father *upon* you." And then He reinforces that it is an *outward, "upon,"* experience because He said, "But you are to stay in the city until you are *clothed* with power from on high."

Clothing is something that we wear on the *outside*. We don't wear clothing on the *inside*; clothing is worn on the *outside*. And so He was speaking about the Baptism in the Holy Spirit that would take place not many days from then. And this—the Baptism in the Holy Spirit—He called "the promise of the Father." So it is clear that "the promise of the Father" was not referring to the working of the Holy Spirit in regeneration or salvation, wherein the Holy Spirit came to take up residence *within* the human spirit, but rather He was talking about the power of God coming *upon* these already saved believers and *clothing* them with *power* from on high.

Now the writer of that Gospel wherein that dissertation in which Jesus told them to wait for the promise of the Father took place was Luke. Luke was also the writer of the Book of Acts. And, in his second book, Luke recounts again the last dissertation of Jesus prior to His ascension. We read that in Acts 1:1-8. There, Luke writes, "The first account I composed, Theophilus, about all that Jesus began to do and teach, until the day when He was taken up to heaven." So, he is saying here, that the first account, what became known as the Gospel of Luke, was all about what Jesus began to do and teach until He was taken up into Heaven, "*after* He had by the Holy Spirit given orders to the apostles whom He had chosen."

Implicit in what Luke says is the fact that this second account, the Book of The Acts of the Apostles, is about what took place *after* that Jesus was taken up into Heaven. However, he begins that book by recounting again the last dissertation of Jesus *prior* to His ascension. And, He says in verse four, "And gathering them together, He commanded them not to leave Jerusalem, but to wait for what the Father had promised, 'Which,' He said, 'you heard of from Me.'"

In this account, Luke adds some crucial details that did not appear in his synoptic book, the Gospel of Luke. In verses 4 and 5, he includes Jesus' interpretation of the phrase, "The promise of the Father," He invoked in Luke's first account, saying that they would be baptized in the Holy Spirit not many days hence: "For John baptized you with water, but you will be baptized with the Holy Spirit not many days from now." And then he goes on to say:

> And so when they had come together, they were asking Him, saying, "Lord, is it at this time You are restoring the kingdom to Israel?" He said to them, "It is not for you to know times or epochs which the Father has fixed by His own authority; **but you shall receive power when the Holy Spirit has come upon you;** and you shall be witnesses both in Jerusalem and in Judea, and in Samaria, and even to the remotest part of the earth."

Jesus here is clearly and explicitly defining the promise of the Father as being *The Baptism in the Holy Spirit*, not *salvation* as some teachers purport. In verse 8, Jesus explains that the effect of the Baptism in the Holy Spirit will be that the disciples would receive supernatural *power* to bear witness of the resurrected Christ, in contrast to the *fruit* of the

Spirit that Born Again believers receive in regeneration of the Spirit.

An Adjunctive Experience

Now, the truth I'm going to establish from Scripture in this section is that the Baptism in the Holy Spirit is an adjunctive—that is, something that is associated with but yet separate and distinct from—the experience of regeneration or salvation.

To establish that point, I want to talk to you about what happened on Resurrection Sunday (aka, *Easter*) *evening*. In the Christian Church, many celebrate what took place on Resurrection *morning*. And, certainly, that glorious fact and event needs to be celebrated and is worthy of great celebration, because it is at that time that the disciples found that the tomb was empty, though that should not really have been a surprise since Jesus prophesied He would rise again on the third day. However, what took place between that morning and that evening culminating in the Upper Room is also of vital importance, and something that we have very little understanding and teaching about in the Christian Church at large.

In John 20:19-23, the story reads, "So when it was *evening* on that day (this is talking about Resurrection Sunday *night*), the first day of the week, and when the doors were shut where the disciples were, for fear of the Jews, Jesus came and stood in their midst and said to them, 'Peace be with you!'" Peace be with you! These were the opening remarks that Jesus made after having ascended into Heaven as the High Priest. Time and space will not allow us to go into all the detail of that—of what took place during the day after Mary had had her encounter with Jesus, in which she attempted to embrace Him but Jesus stopped her and said, "Touch Me not, woman, for I have not yet ascended unto My Father."

He was speaking about the fact, that He was about to ascend into Heaven as our spiritual High Priest, and as it was written, a priest serving in the role of High Priest, after

He had been purified through the purification rites God had prescribed, in order not to defile himself, must avoid all human contact, i.e., the touching or being touched by *any* human, but especially a woman. For while He had ascended from the regions of hell by means of the resurrection power of the Holy Spirit that would later come upon them and thereby "quicken" their mortal bodies, He said, "Receive ye the Holy Spirit." And that was the first time that *anyone* was ever born again.

These 120 disciples who were gathered together in the Upper Room were born again at that point. They received of the regenerative working of the Holy Spirit at that moment in the manner that we today receive of that regenerative working of the Holy Spirit when we accept Jesus as our personal Lord and Savior. Jesus comes to live in our hearts, our sins are forgiven, thereby reconciling us with God, and we become alive with the Life of the Holy Spirit, as He takes up residence within our human spirit.

But, then, what we are going to see next is how the same believers who are now spiritually alive in their human spirit through the workings of the regenerative power of God, infused with the *Life* of God in their human spirit, had a second and adjunctive, a separate and distinct, another experience with the Holy Spirit some days afterward, in which they received, not the *Life* of God, but they were imbued with *power* from on high—which Jesus defined as *"the promise of the Father"* (Ac. 1:4).

Separate, Distinct Workings of the Spirit

Summarizing briefly, in previous segments, we established conclusively and incontrovertibly from Scripture that the Baptism in the Holy Spirit is a separate and distinct, or adjunctive, experience to the infusion of the Holy Spirit that transpires at the moment of salvation. To state it another way, regeneration by the Spirit in salvation, the New Birth, and the Baptism in the Holy Spirit are two distinct and separate workings of the Holy Spirit that perform different works and impart different benefits.

In salvation, the Holy Spirit comes to live *within* the believer, becoming in the believer a well of water springing *up*—in contrast to *out*—unto Eternal Life, Jesus explained in John 4:14. This is the regenerative work of the Holy Spirit at the moment of salvation, wherein the Holy Spirit takes up residence in the previously dead human spirit, connecting the person with God, imparting the Life of God, and thereby causing the believer to become a partaker of the Divine Nature, as Peter stated in Second Peter 1:4, along with the accompanying attributes of God, that is, the nine *fruit* of the Spirit, enumerated in Galatians 5:22 and 23. It is the presence of these fruit in the life of the believer that gives evidence and testimony to the fact that a person has indeed been born again by the living and abiding Word of God and through the supernatural regenerative work of the Holy Spirit in salvation.

However, in the Baptism in the Holy Spirit, the believer is enveloped by, or immersed in, the Holy Spirit. That is to say, the Holy Spirit comes *upon* the believer, in contrast to *into* the believer, encompassing, or overshadowing, the born-again, or regenerated, human spirit that has been infused with the Holy Spirit, and supercharges the believer with the *dunamis-power* of God, rather than the *Life* of God, imparting upon the born-again child of God the nine supernatural *gifts* of the Holy Spirit, also called "the manifestations of the Spirit," which are enumerated in First Corinthians 12:8-10. These manifestations of the Spirit are inherent in the Living Waters that Jesus said, in John 7:37-39, would **flow** *out of*, as opposed to being **contained** *in* the "innermost being," or human spirit, of those who believe in Him and been regenerated, or born again, by the infusion of the Spirit into their previously spiritually dead human spirit. Verse 39 states, "But this He spoke of the Spirit, whom those *who believed* in Him were to receive; for the Spirit was not yet given, because Jesus was not yet glorified."

Now, while regeneration by the Spirit and empowerment by the Spirit are two separate and distinct workings or transactions of the Spirit, that is not to say that they cannot occur at the same time. Indeed, there are instances in the Bible where these transactions occurred contemporaneously, meaning at the same time. And, I have personally witnessed this double blessing, if you will, occurring many times in my experience and ministry, that is to say, people were saved and baptized in the Spirit at the same time. I have also personally witnessed people being baptized in water and in the Spirit at the same time, wherein they came up out of the water worshiping God in a language unknown to them.

Nevertheless, contemporaneous occurrence of these transactions of the Spirit does not indicate that these transactions are the *same* transaction, or that they are *not* separate and distinct.

To illustrate, as a former baseball umpire, I many times witnessed one form of what is known as a "double play," when with a runner occupying a base, an infielder caught a line drive, while simultaneously stepping on the base that the runner had vacated while attempting to advance toward the next base, before the runner was able to return to the base. The catching of the line drive retired the batsman, for one out; and the contacting of the base by the infielder with the ball in his possession with the runner off the base retired the runner for the second out. Voilà! A double play!

However, each of those actions by the offensive player was a separate and distinct transaction, even though in that case, they occurred simultaneously. A player catching a line drive and contacting a base does not *always* produce a double play, but only in the case of a "force out." These are separate and distinct transactions that *can* occur simultaneously, but are not *required* to occur simultaneously in order to effect the outcome each transaction effects.

Typology of Israel and the Two Baptisms

"For I do not want you to be unaware, brethren, that our fathers were **all under the** cloud **and all passed through the** sea; **and all were baptized into Moses** in the cloud and in the sea; and all ate the same spiritual food; and all drank the same spiritual drink, for they were drinking from a spiritual rock which followed them; and the rock was Christ." (1 Cor. 10:1-4)

The Israelites, according to what the Apostle Paul is pointing out in the above passage, experienced two separate and distinct baptisms or immersions into Moses, who was a type of Christ. This is a description of Biblical typology that symbolizes the two separate and distinct workings of the Holy Spirit in the lives of believers that God expects all believers to undergo. Paul told the Corinthians he did not want them to be unaware of this fact that the Israelites were ALL **under the cloud** of God's glory and presence—i.e., His Spirit—that manifest all throughout their forty-year trek through the Wilderness after being delivered out of 430 years of bondage in Egypt, which is a symbol of the kingdom of Satan, and they "**ALL passed through the sea**" when they were delivered. And all this was a part of their experience of being "baptized in to Moses," who, as I said, was a type of Christ to them.

Their having "passed through the sea" is a reference of passing through the Red Sea, which is a type of the Blood of Christ by which all believers are redeemed, as well as the Living Waters of God in regeneration, which correlates to water baptism for the forgiveness of sins, as John the Baptist baptized people as a testimony of repentance during his forerunner ministry preparing the way for the manifestation of the Christ or Messiah.

Whereas, them **all** having been "under the cloud" is symbolic of the Baptism in the Holy Spirit, in that the cloud was the *presence* of God by day, and the pillar of fire by night was representative of God's *essence* by night, for our God is a consuming fire!" (Heb. 12:29). This also correlates to what John the Baptist said concerning Jesus, "As for me, I baptize you with water for repentance, but He who is coming after me is mightier than I, and I am not fit to remove His sandals; He will baptize you with the **Holy Spirit and fire**" (Mat. 3:11).

As they followed Moses, the Israelites were first delivered, set free, and given a new life of freedom from the bondage of their slave-masters and Pharaoh, by passing through the Red Sea, through which their former captors could not pass, typifying the deliverance, liberation, and regeneration, or New Life, believers in Christ experience. Then, during their forty-years in the wilderness they experienced daily the cloud by day and the fire by night, both manifestations in which God was demonstrating His constant and abiding presence in and providence over their lives. The former symbolized the regeneration and daily rejuvenation by the Spirit that the Israelites experienced and believers in Christ experience. The latter symbolized the empowerment inuring from anointing of the Spirit of God over the Israelites and believers. Both—regeneration of the Spirit and the empowerment of the anointing—were/are needed and necessary.

This all correlates to what occurred with the first disciples. They were born again, regenerated, in the Upper Room on Resurrection Evening, but nevertheless Jesus commanded them to wait in Jerusalem until they were "endued with power from on high" (Lk. 24:49). They were born again and changed into new creatures in Christ, the internal workings of the Spirit was accomplished, but their ministry to others could not begin until the Holy Spirit had empowered and equipped them—anointed them—as He later did on the Day of Pentecost.

So also it is with every believer, the overriding issue now that one is born again is, as Paul asked the Ephesian believers, "Did you receive the Holy Spirit (baptism) *since* you believed?" (Ac. 19:2; KJV). He did not question whether or not they were believers and therefore saved, regenerated, born again. He obviously knew these men were genuine believers. Rather, what concerned him and impelled his question to them was their obvious lack of power. Indeed, this scenario underscores the fact that regeneration does not equip or empower us for ministry. Rather, Spirit-baptism or Spirit-immersion does. A well is not a river! A well is a *container* of water, but a river is a *conduit* of water! Both are needed and necessary, but one is for the individual and the other is for others to whom the waters of the Spirit flow! The Red Sea is needed and necessary, and where it all begins, but the Cloud by day and the Fire by night is where it all leads!

Lest the point be lost in the intricacies of the symbology, let me reiterate that the main point of this portion of teaching is that the aforecited passage of Scripture is more proof of the overall point that the working of the Holy Spirit in regeneration and the working of the Spirit in baptism in the Holy Spirit are separate and distinct, or adjunctive, workings of the same Holy Spirit; both necessary and needed; one for personal salvation and the other for ministry unto others.

The Holy Spirit's Dual Work in Jesus and Us: Conception and Anointing

Before I leave this line of teaching, I want to share some thoughts relative to this matter of the two separate and distinct workings of the Holy Spirit from my dear friend Pastor Charles Carrin, in which he speaks of them in terms of *conception* and *anointing*. I will share more about Charles and his remarkable ministry history as well as some more quotes from him in Chapters 14 and 15. What follows here to the end of this chapter is an excerpt from one of his recent newsletters.

[*Begin Charles Carrin excerpt*] ...As with Moses in Egypt, killing the Passover Lamb and putting its blood in the basin did not deliver Israel. The blood had to be applied to the doorpost of each person being saved. Without the application of the blood, the Israelite's firstborn would have died with the Egyptians. Identically for us, the blood of Jesus must be applied personally to each one. It is this fact which necessitated the Holy Spirit's second work in Jesus. By that, I refer to the anointing that came upon Jesus in the Jordan and which initiated His public ministry.

The two works of the Spirit Jesus experienced were:

Conception and *Anointing*. Conception occurred in the womb of the Virgin Mary and Anointing occurred during His baptism in the Jordan River. One without the other would have left His mission incomplete. Jesus' conception by the Spirit was for the purpose of His incarnation and redemption; the angel explained this to Mary, "The Holy Spirit will come upon you, and the power of the Highest will overshadow you; therefore, also, that Holy One who is to be born will be called the Son of God'" (Lk. 1:35). In calming Joseph's fears about Mary's pregnancy, the same angel said, "She will bring forth a Son, and you shall call His name JESUS, for He will save His people from their sins" (Mat. 1:21). The work of conception pointed toward the Cross and redemption.

Jesus' anointing by the Spirit imparted the miraculous power needed for His public ministry. He explained this in His first sermon in Nazareth immediately following His baptism when He said,

> "The Spirit of the LORD is upon Me, Because He has anointed Me to preach the gospel to the poor; He has sent Me to heal the brokenhearted, to proclaim liberty to the captives and recovery of sight to the blind, to set at liberty those who are oppressed; to proclaim the acceptable year of the LORD." (Lk. 4:18-19)

Prior to His anointing, Jesus healed no sickness, cast out no demon, performed no miracle. That changed immediately with the Spirit's descent upon Him.

To be thorough students of the Word, we must be theologically confirmed in both aspects of the Holy Spirit's ministry in Jesus. Conception equipped Him for the Cross and Mankind's redemption; Anointing equipped Him for the miraculously endowed works of the gospel. Not only so, but we must realize that the Holy Spirit has more purpose for us than just our new-birth/conception. We too urgently need His anointing. Much of modern Christianity ignores this vital truth. [*End Charles Carrin excerpt*]

* * * *

The Spirit's Work in Spirit Baptism 53

All these truths concerning these two separate and distinct workings of the Holy Spirit in regeneration and empowerment of believers are clearly supported by Scripture and exemplified by the experience of Jesus Himself, who is our ultimate Model, as well as the experience of the first disciples of the Early Church. Moreover, though they have been well established already in this volume, the remainder of the book is dedicated to providing additional proof from Scripture that further corroborate these truths.

Chapter Six
Tongues — The Initial Evidence

Over the course of this volume thus far I've been leading you on a journey to discover the *Real Truth* about a matter second in importance none, except salvation itself, which is the matter of the Baptism in the Holy Spirit. Each segment of teaching has been a vital leg of that journey that leads ultimately to the real truth concerning the role of the Third Member of the Godhead, in your life, whom Jesus Himself called, "The Helper," that is, the blessed Holy Spirit, the Living Waters of God.

Now, in this segment of teaching, we will examine the Biblical initial evidence that someone has received the Baptism in the Holy Spirit, which is the gift of tongues, that is, a supernatural enablement to speak in languages that the speaker has never learned. This is referred to in the Bible as *unknown tongues*. It is called *unknown tongues*, again, because the languages, or tongues (*glossa*, Gr.) the Spirit-Baptized believer speaks are unknown to the speaker. It is not that the tongue is not known by *anyone*, but rather, it is not known, or understood, or has been learned, by the *speaker*. In fact, in many cases — and for all that can be determined definitively (and I personally believe, though obviously cannot provide proof-positive), in *every* case — the language that the Spirit-baptized believer is speaking is indeed a "known" language or dialect *somewhere* and by *some* anthropological people or race extant upon the Earth somewhere. Moreover, historically, there have been recorded incidences when Spirit-baptized believers have spoken publicly in a tongue unknown to the speaker, either in the form of prayer and praise or as a prophetic word (then interpreted), and the language spoken was the native language of or known by the others who heard the outward expression. Such an occurrence is sometimes referred to as, *glossolalia*, based on the Greek word for speaking in tongues.

We will examine the matter of speaking in tongues itself in Chapter Thirteen, but our main focus here is *tongues* as the initial evidence that someone has received the Baptism in the Holy Spirit. In every case in which believers are reported to have received the Baptism in the Holy Spirit in the Bible, the initial evidence, or indicator, or sign, of their having received it was that they spoke in tongues unknown to them. Moreover, there is no instance recorded in the Bible in which believers received the Baptism in the Holy Spirit without receiving and manifesting the gift of *tongues* as the initial evidence of having received it. Although, there is one incident, which we will examine later, in which it is not explicitly stated that those believers baptized in the Spirit spoke in tongues; but there is, however, implicit and historic evidence that they *did*, and no definitive historic evidence has ever been presented that they did *not*. From the preponderance of Scriptural record, it is extremely, and in fact, unimpeachably safe, to conclude that the Biblical pattern of the initial sign or indicator that a person has received the Baptism in the Holy Spirit is speaking in tongues. Certainly, it's safer to say it *is*, than that it's *not*.

I'll even take it a step further and say that since the Holy Spirit is Himself the true *Inspiration* behind every word of Scripture (2 Tim. 3:16), and that He can be aptly described, based on what He does, as the *Expression* and ultimate *Spokesman* of God, it appears by this pattern firmly fixed in Scripture that a verbal eruption or bubbling forth of Rivers of Living Water in human language through a believer who has just experienced Immersion in the Holy Spirit is the form in which the Holy Spirit expresses or vocalizes the worship, praise, and adulation of God of which He consists in such moments. It's as if torrents of Rivers of Living Waters of God, in the moment of the Baptism in the Holy Spirit, are suddenly and finally bursting through and overruning the dam that has pent them up in the human vessel who has now released the oceans of the Spirit to come forth!

Because He is the Expression of God, language and the Holy Spirit are inextricably connected. So when you are talking about "tongue-talking," you are actually talking about the Holy Spirit. As referenced repeatedly throughout this volume, while it is the Spirit-baptized believer who is the human agent or vehicle He is using to speak through, the source of the substance or essence of what is being articulated when a believer is speaking in tongues is the Holy Spirit! That being so, it is therefore possible to be engaging in "blasphemy against the Holy Spirit" when maligning or ridiculing the matter of speaking in tongues, particularly when attributing it to the devil, which Jesus specifically warned was an eternal sin that shall never be forgiven:

> "Therefore I say to you, any sin and blasphemy shall be forgiven people, but blasphemy against the Spirit shall not be forgiven. "Whoever speaks a word against the Son of Man, it shall be forgiven him; but whoever speaks against the Holy Spirit, it shall not be forgiven him, either in this age or in the age to come." (Mat. 12:31-32)

More disconcerting with respect to the myriad of "resisters of the Holy Spirit," is that it is hardly necessary to point out that unforgiven sin is what separates Mankind from God eternally, and no one with unconfessed and therefore unforgiven sin can possibly have eternal fellowship and communion with God, which would mean eternal separation from God and everlasting damnation.

Critics and Resisters of the Holy Spirit

Some critics of this line of teaching, who invariably, in my experience, have never themselves had a release of the "rivers of living water," as Jesus described it, in the form of tongues (meaning they've never spoken in tongues themselves), vehemently and vociferously reject and vainly attempt to repudiate these assertions. Such naysayers are of that category of deluded religionists Stephen identified as *Resisters of the Holy Spirit*: "You men who are stiff-necked and uncircumcised in heart and ears *are always resisting the Holy Spirit*; you are doing just as your fathers did" (Ac. 7:51). Indeed, it was over the initial outpouring of the Holy Spirit upon the first 120 believers who all spoke in unknown tongues that the great persecution against the Early Church arose, which demonstrates in no uncertain terms the magnitude of the hatred and contempt for the Holy Spirit of God, the Third Member of the Godhead, with which unbelieving and Spirit-resisting religionists are possessed. More often than not the varying degrees of contempt for tongues and the Baptism in the Spirit with which Christian-claiming critics of the Baptism in the Holy and its accompanying speaking in tongues are possessed is predicated in pride and arrogance and a lack of genuine personal brokenness commonly manifest with espousal of "intellectual Christianity," which is the product of mental assent of the Gospel vis-à-vis the regenerative workings of the Holy Spirit in a genuine Born Again believer's heart and life.

Now tongues are by no means the *only* sign of the Baptism of the Holy Spirit, but they are the *initial* sign of the Baptism in the Holy Spirit. Indeed, the Apostle Paul tells us, in First Corinthians 14:22, that "Tongues are for a *sign* to unbelievers," meaning an indicator testifying of the supernatural power of God manifested through the speaker. Tongues are not the Baptism itself, but rather tongues are an expression of the Holy Spirit through the Spirit-Immersed believer. Tongues are a part of the Baptism in the Spirit; they are not separate and distinct from the Holy Spirit. Tongues are an expression of the Holy Spirit, not the believer speaking. One does not merely receive tongues with the Baptism in the Holy Spirit; rather tongues are an outflow of the Spirit Himself, not the believer. As with the 120 and then 3,000 more on the Day of Pentecost, the believer provides the vocalization, but the substance of the vocalization, comes from the Holy Spirit: "And *they* were all filled with the Holy Spirit and (they) began to speak with other tongues, **as the Spirit was giving them utterance**"

(Ac. 2:4). The believer yields his/her tongue to the Holy Spirit, who provides the substance of the utterance.

The way I like to explain it, and have done so in many meetings where I ministered the Baptism in the Holy Spirit to many who received it as easily as drinking a glass of water, is that it's like this: When you buy a pair of shoes, the tongue comes with it! You don't buy a pair of shoes and then have to buy a pair of tongues to go with the shoes. The tongues come part and parcel with the shoes. Tongues are part and parcel of the Holy Spirit and the Immersion in the Spirit. To refuse or reject the Baptism in the Holy Spirit and the tongues He expresses through Spirit-Baptized believers is to refuse and reject the *Person* of the Holy Spirit.

The Day of Pentecost

Now the first of these incidences we want to examine is that of the initial outpouring of the Holy Spirit on the Day of Pentecost, which occurred fifty days after Jesus' resurrection. We actually made tangential reference to this incident in previous segments, when we were establishing other points about the Baptism in the Holy Spirit. In those segments, we established the fact that the original disciples were saved through the regenerative working of the Holy Spirit on Resurrection Evening, when Jesus appeared unto them in the Upper Room, announcing and pronouncing *peace* between them and God the Father, and proceeded to breathe upon them, saying to them, "Receive the Holy Spirit." It was at this moment that the disciples were all infused with the Holy Spirit in their previously dead human spirit, giving life to it, and filling it with the Holy Spirit.

But it was forty days after this, on the Day of Ascension, ten days before the Day of Pentecost, that Jesus gathered the disciples together, and according to Luke's account in Acts 1:4–5:

> He commanded them not to leave Jerusalem, but to wait for what the Father had promised, "Which," He said, "you heard of from Me; for John baptized with water, but you will be baptized with the Holy Spirit not many days from now."

He went on to explain to them on that occasion that they would receive power when the Holy Spirit would come upon them—that is, when they were baptized with the Holy Spirit—and that the purpose and function of that power would be to make them effective witnesses of Him.

One translation explicitly says, "When the Holy Spirit comes upon you, you shall receive *power to **testify** of Me with **great effect**.*" Indeed, that is the purpose of the Baptism in the Holy Spirit, to empower believers to testify of the resurrected Christ with *great effect*, that is, with supernatural and effectual testimony. Indeed, in his first account, Luke writes that Jesus said to the disciples, "You are *witnesses* of these things. And, behold, I am sending forth the promise of the Father upon you; but you are to stay in the city until you are clothed with power from on high." The Baptism in the Holy Spirit is all about being clothed with supernatural power from on high that gives effectual and irrefutable testimony of Jesus and His resurrection as well as His resurrection power.

Not many days later, as He had said, ten to be precise, following His ascension into Heaven, on the Day of Pentecost, the initial outpouring of the Holy Spirit occurred. In Acts 2:1(ff), we read:

> "When the Day of Pentecost had come, they were all together in one place. And suddenly there came from Heaven a noise like a violent rushing wind and it filled the whole house where they were sitting. And there appeared to them tongues of as a fire distributing themselves, and they rested on each one of them. And they were all filled with the Holy Spirit and began to speak with other tongues, as the Spirit was giving them utterance. Now there were Jews living in Jerusalem, devout men, from every nation under Heaven. And when this sound occurred, the crowds came together, and were bewildered, because each one of them was hearing them speak in his own language."

Now we can see from this incident on the Day of Pentecost, as with so many other incidences in the Bible, the

Almighty's affinity for compelling theatrical staging. When God wants to make a point, He certainly knows how to make that point in a way that is unequivocal and unmistakable. Surely, with the appearance of tongues as of fire distributing themselves and resting on each one of these early disciples, God was demonstrating that with the outpouring of the Holy Spirit upon believers comes a manifestation of the gift of tongues. And the result of those tongues of fire that rested upon each one of those disciples was that they were all filled or supercharged with the Holy Spirit, and they began to speak with other tongues as the Spirit was giving them utterance.

They Spoke and the Spirit Gave the Utterance

Now it is important to understand and to extract from this text the fact that amid all the controversy surrounding this matter of speaking in tongues, it was *they*, the disciples, who "began to speak with other tongues." They surrendered and submitted their tongue, which is one of the great benefits of the Baptism in the Holy Spirit—the ability to surrender and submit your tongue under the lordship of Jesus Christ. *They themselves* began to speak. And what they were speaking was a language that they had not previously known, as the Spirit was giving them utterance. It was the Spirit who was giving them the *substance* of what they were uttering, but it was *they* who were doing the *speaking*, using their speech faculties to speak the Spirit's utterances.

And what they were speaking was not vain babble and gibberish, as some anti-tongues teachers allege "tongue-talkers" are engaging in, but rather the Bible explicitly says that those who were standing by *heard* them speaking in *languages* that they themselves understood. Yet they also understood that these people did not understand those languages and dialects in which they were speaking just nanoseconds prior to the outpouring, indicating that this was a supernatural working of the Holy Spirit as a *sign* to those that were unbelievers—a *sign* that clearly testified of the supernatural power of God being poured out upon these believers in Christ.

So, we can see clearly from this first incident on the Day of Pentecost that tongues is the Biblical *initial* evidence that someone has received the Baptism in the Holy Spirit.

In the segments that follow, we will examine other incidences that also demonstrate that incontrovertible fact.

Speaking in Tongues is the Second Tenet of the "Great Commission"

It is vital to understand with respect to this matter of speaking in tongues that it is the second tenet of The Great Commission Jesus issued to the Church:

> And He said to them, "Go into all the world and preach the gospel to all creation. "He who has believed and has been baptized shall be saved; but he who has disbelieved shall be condemned. "These signs will accompany those who have believed: in My name they will cast out demons, **they will speak with new tongues**; they will pick up serpents, and if they drink any deadly poison, it will not hurt them; they will lay hands on the sick, and they will recover." (Mk. 16:15-18)

Today, in the 21st Century, more than two-thousand years since Jesus charged the Church collectively and believers individually with these words—what has come to be known as "The Great Commission," the five tenets of which it consists–have been essentially relegated to the lowest of priorities in the vast majority of churches, and sadly are manifest less and less in churches, including those who claim to espouse Pentecostal or Charismatic belief systems. In fact, the higher the order in Jesus' charge, the lesser place it has in most churches in this hour. I deal with the void in most churches of casting out of demons—the first tenet of The Great Commission, in my book, *Deliverance From Demonic Powers*. Believers speaking in tongues is the second tenet, and I believe Jesus spoke of them in the order of their priority to the church and believers. Yet, in these end-times in which we are now living—times requiring more manifestation of God's supernatural power than ever before in history—more and more, speaking in tongues is being eschewed or outright rejected by those claiming to be believers and whole denominations of churches, despite that they are the expressions of the Holy Spirit, not people.

It is a sad and discouraging scenario to see such spiritually impotent individual believers and whole churches in this hour; and unnecessarily so. It is as a preacher recently said, that if you were somehow able to assemble all the so-called "spirit-filled" and "full-gospel" believers in America in one massive stadium, they wouldn't have enough power accumulatively to blow their nose! Of course, that is an exaggeration to make the point of how powerless believers are today, despite the fact that every one of us have at our disposal the same power that Jesus was immersed in at the Jordan River when the Holy Spirit descended upon Him, and from that very hour forward, after triumphing over forty days and forty nights in the wilderness being tempted by the devil, He went out to begin His public ministry of miracles, signs, wonders, and displays of supernatural power—Dunamis-Power!

> Jesus was going throughout all Galilee, teaching in their synagogues and *proclaiming the gospel of the kingdom*, and **healing every kind of disease and every kind of sickness among the people.** (Mat. 4:23)
>
> Jesus was going through all the cities and villages, teaching in their synagogues and *proclaiming the gospel of the kingdom*, and **healing every kind of disease and every kind of sickness.** (Mat. 9:35)

The significance of the fact that Jesus Himself did not perform even a single miracle before He was baptized in the Holy Spirit cannot be overemphasized. Not one miracle!

Notice also in the above verses that demonstration of supernatural power was part and parcel of the Gospel of the Kingdom that Jesus preached. It still is. The Kingdom is the same as then; thus the Gospel of the Kingdom is the same as then. And, Scripture definitively declares that the Jesus who preached that Gospel is still the same as well: "Jesus Christ is the same yesterday and today and forever" (Heb. 13:8). That is true because that is what Jesus said in another record of "The Great Commission" Jesus issued to the Church He is building for all ages until He returns and gathers us together in the air to be eternally united with Him:

> And Jesus came up and spoke to them, saying, "All authority has been given to Me in heaven and on earth. "Go therefore and **make disciples** of all the nations, baptizing them in the name of the Father and the Son and the Holy Spirit, **teaching them to observe all that I commanded you**; and lo, I am with you always, even to the end of the age." (Mat. 28:18-20)

His command was to make *disciples*, which means learners, but not just people who learn, but also, by definition, disciples are people who learn **and obey**, as He said, "teaching them to **observe** (obey) all that I commanded you." And, one of the things Jesus commanded the early disciples, but then, by extension every disciple from then to the present day, is to "wait…for the promise of the father" before they went out to minister as His witnesses:

> And, being assembled together with them, **commanded them** that they should not depart from Jerusalem, but wait for the promise of the Father, which, saith he, "ye have heard of me. For John truly baptized with water; but ye shall be baptized with the Holy Ghost not many days hence." (Ac. 1:4-5; KJV)

Moreover, that "promise of the father" He **commanded** them to wait on and receive was, as we have shown in various places in this volume, the Baptism in the Holy Spirit that was first poured out on the Day of Pentecost. Just as The Great Commission is not The Great Suggestions, but a list of commandments, so also Jesus' charge for every believer to be baptized in the Holy Spirit is a *command*, not merely a good *suggestion*.

Another compelling fact relative to Jesus' command in the Matthew 28 passage cited above to "make disciples" is that as He commanded the early disciples, "Come and follow me," that is also the command to every disciple since then, i.e., to follow the model that Jesus set. As discussed in other portions of this teaching, Jesus is the Heavenly Prototype sent from God to be our model for "everything pertaining to life and godliness" (2 Pet. 1:3), and He Himself first received the Baptism in the Holy Spirit before He began His ministry. Thus, every believer should follow His example and be immersed in the Spirit as Jesus was in order to allow the outflow of the Spirit to be the source of all we do in the name of "ministry."

Additionally, Jesus also commanded all believers in all ages to perform not only the supernatural works of power that He performed, but even greater works:

> "Truly, truly, I say to you, **he who believes in Me**, the works that I do, **he will do also**; and **greater works** than these he will do; because I go to the Father." (Jn. 14:12)

Again, Jesus was the Model for all ministry, and His ministry was accompanied with supernatural works of power, and He expects every believer to perform the works He performed and even greater works, "because I go to the Father," which means two things: one, He will no longer be here on Earth to do the works Himself, and He is now sitting at the right hand of God evermore making intercession on behalf of the saints unto the Father (Heb. 7:25). We are now His body, his hands, his feet, his mouth, to perform *His* works on His behalf—continuing and carrying on *His* ministry! Hallelujah! What an honor and privilege is ours!

Three Primary Objections to Tongues

There are three primary objections people make to the matter of tongues that I won't take a lot of time and space answering here, mainly because they are so manifestly ludicrous from both a Biblical and logical standpoint. All three can be easily countered and dispelled. I will deal briefly with two in this chapter and the third—"Tongues ceased"—will be answered in a more thorough fashion than the other two in Chapter Fourteen.

The first objection I'll deal with here is: "Tongues are of the devil." All the Apostles of the Lamb were present (with the exception of Judas who hanged himself, though his replacement, Mathias was there) on the Day of Pentecost and were partakers of the original outpouring of the Spirit when "they were **all** filled with the Holy Ghost, and began to speak with other tongues, as the Spirit gave them utterance (Ac. 2:4). So if tongues is of the devil then all the Apostles of the Lamb were of the devil because they ALL spoke in tongues.

Moreover, all the New Testament writers were tongue-talkers, including Paul, who wrote two-thirds of the New Testament epistles, and stated categorically that he spoke in tongues more than all the Corinthian believers (1 Cor. 14:18), thus, if tongues is of the devil, so also were all the New Testament writers, particularly Paul, or at least they were all deceived by the devil and spoke in tongues that were inspired by him.

Indeed, looking at what Paul said by inspiration of the Spirit in his first letter to the Corinthians we see him saying that tongues is very much of the Spirit of God, not the devil. First, in verse 13 of Chapter 14, Paul writes: "Therefore let one who **speaks** *in a tongue* pray that he may interpret." Here Paul is talking about a message inspired of the Holy Spirit expressed through a believer in an assembly of believers that is one-half of prophecy (more on this in Chapter Thirteen). Notice the word "speaks"; he is talking here about *speaking* in tongues, not an individual *praying* in tongues. His instruction here is that tongues spoken in a public forum must be interpreted into the common language of those gathered, so that those present can understand the message from God.

Then, in the 14th verse, He talks about praying in the Spirit, and says, "For if I pray *in a tongue*, my spirit prays, but my mind is unfruitful." He is saying that when a believer prays in tongues, it is his/her spirit, infused as it is with the Holy Spirit, that is actually doing the praying by the inspiration of the Spirit, rather than the believer praying with his/her intellect, because his/her "mind is unfruitful." So, for tongues to be of the devil that would mean that the Holy Spirit is praying through the inspiration of the devil as He petitions God through the believer who is praying in tongues. Obviously, that is also a literal impossibility!

Finally, the Apostle Paul in his teaching of the Corinthians enumerates "various kinds of tongues" as one of the nine manifestations of the Spirit (charismata) that are all for the common *good* of those who are beneficiaries of the gifts:

> But to each one is given the manifestation of the Spirit for the common good. For to one is given the word of wisdom through the Spirit, and to another the word of knowledge according to the same Spirit; to another faith by the same Spirit, and to another gifts of healing by the one Spirit, and to another the effecting of miracles, and to another prophecy, and to another the distinguishing of spirits, to another **various kinds of tongues**, and to another the interpretation of tongues. **But one and the same Spirit works all these things**, distributing to each one individually **just as He wills**. (1 Cor. 12:7-11; NASB)

Take special note of the last sentence of that quote. Paul categorically states that it is the Holy Spirit who works or operates ALL of these nine "manifestations **OF THE SPIRIT**" he delineated. And, he stated that distribution of those giftings is in accordance with His—the Holy Spirit's—will. How can it be that the Holy Spirit operates and distributes all these gifts and yet they be of the devil at the same time. Impossible! Ludicrous! Inane! Senseless! Illogical! Blasphemous!

Additionally, and perhaps the most convincing of all, in Luke 11:9-13, Jesus said this concerning the Holy Spirit in the immersion of the Spirit:

> "So I say to you, ask, and it will be given to you; seek, and you will find; knock, and it will be opened to you. "For everyone who asks, receives; and he who seeks, finds; and to him who knocks, it will be opened. "Now suppose one of you fathers is asked by his son for a **fish**; he will not give him a **snake** instead of a fish, will he? "Or if he is asked for an **egg**, he will not give him a **scorpion**, will he? "If you then, being evil, know how to give good gifts to your children, **how much more will your heavenly Father give the Holy Spirit to those who ask Him?**"

In this dissertation about the Father giving the Holy Spirit to His children who ask Him both the terms "fish" and "egg" are types of elements of the Kingdom of God, and "snake" and "scorpion" are Biblical types of Satan's Kingdom. When you couple what Jesus said here with the word of the Holy Spirit through the Apostle John in his first epistle, for example, concerning receiving from the Father what we ask for that is according to His will, it is clear that Jesus is saying definitively that when any believer asks the Father for something of His Kingdom—in this case, to receive the Baptism in the Holy Spirit—the Father is not going to answer by giving you something from Satan's Kingdom:

> This is the confidence which we have before Him, that, if we ask anything **according to His will**, He hears us. And if we know that He hears us in whatever we ask, we know that we have the requests which we have asked from Him. (1 Jn. 5:14-15)

And since Jesus was relating what He said to receiving the Baptism in the Holy Spirit, we then know conclusively that the Baptism in the Holy Spirit is of the will of God, because He said, "how much more will your heavenly Father give the Holy Spirit to **those who ask Him**?" Indeed, if God were to ever give someone something from Satan's kingdom—the kingdom of darkness—then He would with that act have associated or affiliated Himself, who is **LIGHT**, with Satan and darkness, and He would cease to be Light. Thus, that is an impossibility.

> This is the message we have heard from Him and announce to you, that God is **Light**, and in Him there is **no darkness at all**. (1 Jn. 1:5)

There's much more that could be said to counter this objection but just what *has* been said is sufficient to dispel that notion entirely.

The second objection I'll deal with here is: "Jesus didn't speak in unknown tongues." This is actually the easiest to dispel and debunk by the fact that since Jesus IS the Word (logos) of God (John 1:1-14; 1 Jn. 1:1-3; et al.) "made manifest," and the embodiment or incarnation of the Word of God, and indeed was the Word that was the Source of the entire Creation "In the beginning (Gen. 1:1), He is also the Source of all language in the Creation. Jesus IS the Word! All language is made up of words. Jesus was/is the language of God! Thus, there is no language on Earth, or anywhere else in the Cosmos, for that matter, that is **unknown** to Him! For Jesus to speak in unknown tongues is a literal impossibility! So, that one too is DOA and really makes no sense at all! **OF COURSE** Jesus didn't speak in unknown tongues!

Proof of Supernatural Glossolalia

I remember very vividly an incident that occurred, I believe in 1979, during my early walk as a Christian, that very well illustrated this matter of *glossolalia*, that is, a believer speaking in a language which he or she does not personally know.

One Sunday morning, my wife and I were traveling to church, and while we were some 10 miles or more away from the church that we were going to attend that morning, I saw in my mirror a particular vehicle as it was approaching our vehicle. And for some reason in the Spirit, it got my attention. And I saw two men in the vehicle. Then as the vehicle passed my vehicle in the lane next to the one we were in on this four-lane street, I saw that there were two men in the vehicle, both of them dressed in white shirts and black ties. And as the vehicle passed by, the Holy Spirit said to me, "Those men are preachers," and to my surprise, He continued to say, "And they are going to be in the service this morning." I knew it was the Holy Spirit speaking to me—I was so sure I even said to my wife, "Those men will be in the service this morning"—but I couldn't quite understand why the Holy Spirit would be saying such a thing to me.

However, all of that became clear as the day unfolded. A week or so prior, the pastor had asked me to share in song in that particular service that morning. We arrived at the church; I went to greet the pastor, as is customary prior to a service. And I noticed that the pastor was unusually nervous, and I didn't quite understand why, but I knew it wasn't any of my business, so I proceeded to go out into the sanctuary and take my seat. And in the process of time, the service began, and we were all worshiping the Lord, in song and great worship. But, I did notice that there was quite an unusual anointing of the Holy Spirit present in this service, at least for what had been my previous experience in this particular church.

And, at one point, about fifteen minutes into the worship, I happened to just look over to my right, and in the center aisle, there sat these two men who had passed us in the vehicle earlier on the way to the church. But then, of course, as anyone would, I began to wonder: well, why in the world are they here, who are they, and what does this have to do with anything?

And just a few minutes after that, as the worship was crescendoing up in the Spirit, there came, totally unorchestrated by anyone, a moment of holy silence. And after about thirty seconds or so of that silence, from the very front pew on the left, came a voice from a lady that I could tell was elderly, yet, as she began to speak confidence and boldness began to fill her voice. And she spoke in one of the most beautiful tongues I believe I've ever heard.

But as she was giving that tongue, I also began to feel the stirring, which by then was fairly familiar to me, but by now is much more familiar to me—the stirring of the Holy Spirit within me. And the Holy Spirit began to say to me, from my innermost being, "I am going to give you the interpretation for that tongue." It was an impression that rose up out of my spirit, and I knew that this was what He was saying to me.

But, then, after the tongue ended, and as I was giving a moment for anyone else to interpret it, there came forth an utterance from someone in the congregation; and it was a good edifying word. However, I felt in my spirit as it came forth that this was not the right interpretation of that message in tongues.

And then, strangely, right after that, someone else gave another word to the congregation. However, as that word came forth, I felt in my spirit, that is not the right interpretation of that word that woman gave in tongues either.

And then, after that word, unbelievably, there came forth a *third* word, which I have never before or since heard or seen happen in a service. And I remember thinking within myself, "Well, then, I must be really missing God, because that's the third and there shouldn't be any more than three,"—at least that's what my understanding was at the time.

But, then, to my surprise, the Holy Spirit within me said, "I want you to give that interpretation now." And I remember slightly arguing with the Lord and saying, "But, Lord, there's already been three words given here, plus that tongue itself." But the Lord clearly and strongly answered me and said, "I want you to give that interpretation now." And so, not really knowing what I was going to speak, but knowing that the Lord gives us *a* word, I began to speak, as I customarily do, that one word that I knew that He *was* giving me. And as I did, all of a sudden, a prophetic word began to flow out of me, and I knew it was totally bypassing my mind because I wasn't even thinking any of those things that I said. And out of my innermost-being began to flow, this beautiful and powerful and edifying word of God for this congregation.

And when it was over, the entire congregation just *erupted* in exultation and glorifying worship and praise unto God, which went on for an unusually long period of time. Then, later, when the time came in the service for me to sing my song, I sang my song, and we continued on with the rest of the service.

Well! I had no idea what had really just occurred. Later that afternoon, I received a phone call from the pastor, and in the conversation he began to relate to me what really took place in that meeting. He asked me, "Do you remember those two men that were in the service that sat in such and so place and they were dressed in such and such manner?" I said, "Yes, I remember seeing them, and strangely, before the service as they passed our vehicle, the Lord, said to me, "They're going to be in the service this morning; they are preachers." And the pastor said, "That's right, those two men *are* preachers, and they are officials from my former denomination. They were there in the service, by appointment, and they had asked to come and visit me that day, and they were trying to lure me back into the former denomination that I had been a part of."

Now the thing was that that former denomination that he had been a part of, did not believe in the Baptism in the Holy Spirit, and they do not believe in the manifestations or gifts of the Spirit either. But, those two men that came happen to have been two of the top preachers and scholars in that denomination. And when the service ended, they almost ran to the pastor, and they wanted to talk to him quickly in his study after the service. The pastor said, "I couldn't understand what was going on, because they were so wide-eyed, and seemed to have such an excitement that I had never seen in those men before."

And as they got the pastor in the study, their first question was, "Who was that woman who gave that tongue?" And the pastor responded, "She is one of the longtime members and has been here since the beginning of this church." And they said, "She seems to be just a simple country woman, how is it that she understands Greek?" And the pastor said, "Well, I have known that woman since I've been the pastor here, and I guarantee you that woman does not understand Greek. She's just a simple country woman with little education, who has only a simple understanding of English." But, these pastors said, "But, we heard her speaking in a particular dialect of Greek, of which we are both experts. And she was speaking perfectly in that dialect."

And then, they said, "What about that man who sang the song in the service? The pastor responded, "Yes, I know him, he's a minister, and he was here to bless us in song today at my request." "Well," they asked, "Does he know this dialect of Greek? Does he know the Greek language?" The pastor replied, "Well, he could have studied some Greek in his theology training, but to my knowledge, he doesn't have any special understanding of Greek, or speak it fluently, and certainly not the dialect you're speaking about."

And they said, "Well, we understood every word that that woman was speaking in that tongue that she gave forth. And then, we thought that we had some evidence here that we can prove that this tongues business is not of God, because the first three people who spoke after that woman, none of them said anything having to do at all or even closely resemble what that woman said in her tongue that she spoke forth."

"But, when that man who sang that song spoke and gave his word, it was a *word-for-word* rendering of what that woman had just said in that tongue!"

And they both began to weep before the pastor, and asked God to forgive them for ever thinking that the Baptism in the Holy Spirit and the great gift of tongues was not of God or was of the devil. And both of those men received the Baptism in the Holy Spirit in that pastor's office as he laid hands upon them at their request and prayed for them to receive the Baptism in the Holy Spirit with the initial evidence of speaking in tongues. That day, those two preachers' lives and their theology were thoroughly revolutionized by a demonstration of the supernatural power of God in the form of tongues and interpretation of tongues!

Chapter Seven
The Pauline Example

In this chapter, we will examine yet another example of the gift of *tongues* being bestowed upon a believer who was baptized in the Holy Spirit. The example we want to look at is perhaps one of the most important examples in the Bible, the example of the Apostle Paul, who after he had been baptized in the Holy Spirit, was empowered to write nearly two-thirds of the New Testament as well as to perform many supernatural "signs and wonders and miracles" that he himself identified as "the signs of a true apostle" (2 Cor. 12:12).

Certainly, this one man conveyed to the Church in his letters by far more revelation concerning a wide range of topics than any other New Testament writer. And what many segments of Christendom down through the centuries of church history have failed to understand is that the revelation, understanding, and wisdom that the Apostle Paul supernaturally received through the ability bestowed upon him to convey that revelation as he did, as well as the supernatural workings of power he was empowered to perform during the course of his apostolate, and certainly the extraordinary experiences he was enabled to carry out and endure, were, without any shadow of a doubt, the direct result of his having received the Baptism in the Holy Spirit.

For this account, we're going to look at Acts 9:1-17. However, the story really does not begin there, but rather at the end of the seventh chapter of Acts, with the account of the martyrdom of Stephen, who, we are told, was one of the seven men who were nominated by the congregation to be the first cadre of deacons in the Early Church, who the apostles charged with the task of the administration of serving tables to the widowed believers.

Stephen, we know from history, was one of those who had been baptized in the Holy Spirit on the Day of Pentecost, when the 120 from the Upper Room, plus 3,000 other newly saved believers, were recipients of that original outpouring. The Spirit testifies of Stephen in Acts 6:5 that he was "a man full of faith and of the Holy Spirit." Moreover, verse 8 says, "And Stephen, full of grace and power, was performing great wonders and signs among the people."

Now, whenever there is an extraordinary outpouring of the Spirit of God such as what took place during this beginning period of the Early Church, there is going to be a supernatural backlash launched by Satan in an attempt to counter, and stop, if possible, the move of God. It has always been that way, and will continue to be that way until the Church Age ends with the catching away of the Church at the last trump of God.

Satan always becomes enraged when any believer begins to break out of the dead, lifeless, inert ritualism of religion, and begins to walk in and operate the supernatural enablement and empowerment of the Holy Spirit that comes upon any believer who has received the Baptism in the Holy Spirit, concerning which Jesus testified, "You shall receive power,"—*dunamis,* in the Greek, *dunamis-power*—"after that the Holy Ghost has come upon you" (Ac. 1:8). Stephen was a living, breathing, walking testament of the empowerment that comes from the Baptism in the Holy Spirit, to such a degree that we are told by the Spirit that, "He was full of grace and power," and that he "was performing great wonders and signs among the people" (Ac. 6:8).

We can see throughout the Bible, and especially in the Book of Acts, that whenever the Holy Spirit brings forth a demonstration of the power of God through chosen, anointed, and appointed vessels of God, Satan becomes enraged, and stirs up the religious spirits operating in and through his religious human cooperatives, to bring forth supernatural resistance of the works of God. We know that this was true in the case of Stephen as well, for Acts 6:9 says, "But some men from what was called the Synagogue of the Freemen, including both Cyrenians and Alexandrians, and some from Cilicia and Asia Minor, rose up and argued with Stephen." The next verse tells us, however, that these religious sectarians were unable to cope with the wisdom and the spirit with which he was speaking.

And so the account goes on to tell us that this religious cult secretly induced men to bear false witness against Stephen, and they stirred up the people—the elders and the Scribes and the crowd that gathered—and they rushed Stephen, and dragged him away, and brought him before the Council of the Sanhedrin, where further false witness and charges were made against him.

But, as they were trying to make their case against him, by which they could justify, according to their Jewish laws, their desire to murder him, Stephen became so filled with the Holy Spirit, that his face was literally lit up with the light of the Glory of God, and the Council saw his face as "the face of an angel" (Ac. 6:15)

It can thus be no mere coincidence that when the High Priest queried him for his defense, Stephen began what was the longest recorded message in the Bible, with the story of the Hebrew patriarch Abraham, and how that the God of Glory, he said, appeared to him while he was yet living in Mesopotamia.

Stephen continued with what is one of the most emotionally-rousing sermons recorded in Scripture, telling the Jews present of the long history of rank Jewish disobedience of the very God they claimed for all those centuries to be worshiping, which dissertation ends by saying:

> You men who are stiff-necked and uncircumcised in heart and ears are always resisting the Holy Spirit; you are doing just as your fathers did. Which one of the prophets did your fathers not persecute? And they killed

those who had previously announced the coming of the Righteous One, whose betrayers and murderers you have now become; you who received the law as ordained by angels, and yet did not keep it.

And when the council heard this, they were cut to the quick, became enraged, and began gnashing their teeth at Stephen, and they rushed him, and took off their outer garments, and began stoning Stephen to death.

Where did all this rage come from? Such rage that people are willing to mob and murder a person who is doing nothing but operating under the supernatural empowerment of the Holy Spirit. What was his crime? What had he done? Had he murdered someone, or raped someone's wife, or molested one of their innocent children? Had he stolen from anyone? No! "He was performing great wonders and signs among the people." All of this rage and murder was not really against Stephen, but rather he had nailed it when he said they were stiff-necked resisters of the Holy Spirit. It was the diabolical religious spirits within them that were enraged, and they murdered Stephen, just as they had murdered Jesus. Those religious spirits spoke out in the case of Jesus, after Pilate had vindicated him, saying, *"We* have a law, and by *our* law, he ought to die!" (Jn. 19:7).

Friends, all of you listening to me or reading these words right now, you may be a Christian who has attended church for years and years, you may even be a deacon in your church or even a preacher, but there is something in you that becomes agitated and even enraged by the mere discussion of this whole matter of the Baptism in the Holy Spirit. I guarantee you right now, and I am speaking under the inspiration of the Spirit of God at this very moment, I guarantee you that is not merely *you* that is so enraged, but rather it is a *religious spirit*, and you need to fall down on your knees before God, and beg of Him that He forgive you for your years of resistance to the Holy Spirit, before you cross the line of out-and-out blasphemy against the Holy Spirit, from which there is no return, and no hope of repentance, like Esau who sought for it with tears (Heb. 12:17).

Jesus made it clear that it was blasphemy against the Holy Spirit that is the unforgivable or unpardonable sin, which manifests in the form of religiosity that condemns and mocks the works and manifestations of the Holy Spirit, and attributes it to Beelzebub, or Satan (Mat. 12:31).

Please listen to this lonely cry out of the wilderness today, *repent now*, while there is still time, and while there is still grace being extended to you by the God of all grace!

Now what does this have to do with the matter of the Apostle Paul receiving the Baptism in the Holy Spirit? Well, when the Sanhedrin stripped off their outer robes in order to stone Stephen, there was a young intern who was acting as an aide or attendant at whose feet they laid their garments—his name was Saul, who later became the Apostle Paul (Ac. 7:58). And it was the supremely, selfless, Spirit-inspired act of Stephen, as he was being martyred, that became the seed that years later germinated and bore the fruit of the Apostle to the Gentiles (Rom. 11:13; 1 Tim. 2:7)—when with his dying breath he cried out with a loud voice, and said, "Lord do not hold this sin against them!" (Ac. 7:60). Those sins which you forgive are forgiven; those that you retain are retained, Jesus instructed all the disciples (Jn. 20:23).

This death-bound absolution was what released Saul from his sin of participation in the murder of this true saint of God, and made it possible for him to later have the Damascus Road experience that not only saved his soul, but resulted in the salvation of countless other souls throughout the ages since.

Friend, *this* Steven pronounces absolution from the Throne of Grace for your sin of resistance of the Holy Spirit, in order that you might be released from your guiltiness, and that the scales that have been over your eyes that have been blinding you to the truth regarding the Holy Spirit, can fall from your spiritual eyes, as the scales fell from the eyes of a man named Saul more than 2,000 years ago, so that you might now see the *truth* concerning the Baptism in the Holy Spirit.

Saul—Hebrew of Hebrews Obsessed and Possessed with Murderous Rage

In Acts 8:1, we read that Saul was in hearty agreement with putting Stephen to death. Concerning this, the Apostle Paul, during his first defense before the Jews in Jerusalem, as recorded in Acts 22:19-20, states:

> And I said, "Lord, they themselves understand that in one synagogue after another, I used to imprison and beat those who believed in You. And, when the blood of your witness Stephen was being shed, I also was standing by approving and watching out for the coats of those who were slaying him."

Then, we read in the second part of Acts 8:1,

> "And on that day *(the day on which Stephen was martyred)*, a great persecution began against the Church in Jerusalem, and they were all scattered throughout the regions of Judea and Samaria, except the apostles."

And this man named Saul, who later became the Apostle Paul, was a central figure in this great persecution that arose against the Church, as the Apostle Paul later himself said, in that passage that we looked at previously. In Acts 22:19, he himself said that in one synagogue after another (he) used to imprison and beat those who believed in (Jesus). And then, in Acts 26:9-11, in Paul's third defense before Festus and King Agrippa, the Apostle Paul himself said:

> So then, I thought to myself that I had to do many things *hostile* to the Name of Jesus of Nazareth. And this is just what I did in Jerusalem. Not only did I lock up many of the saints in prisons, having received authority from the chief priest, but also when they were being put to death, I cast my vote against them. And as I punished them often in all of the synagogue I tried to force them to blaspheme and being furiously enraged at them, I kept pursuing them even to foreign cities.

Now, as I indicated previously, this great persecution that arose against those that were members of or part of The Way, as it was called originally—the Church in Jerusalem was called, "The Way," originally—this great persecution that arose, no doubt, was not just a persecution on the human level, rather there were demonic powers in operation in the spirit realm that were behind this great persecution. The spirit of murder had entered into those Sanhedrin who murdered Stephen. Those were evil religious spirits in operation. They were the same religious evil spirits, when He was vindicated by Pilate, who said he could find no wrong in this Man, that He had done nothing wrong, that spoke through those religious people concerning Jesus and said, "*We* have a law, and by *our* law He (Jesus) ought to die" (Jn. 19:7). Friend, that was an evil *murderous* spirit speaking through those religious people concerning their religious "laws" that were based on human religious thinking that were not at all inspired in any way shape or form by God, nor were they predicated on the Word of God in Scripture. Religious spirits *are* murderous spirits!—something that many religious people and churches fail to understand.

Their totally bogus justification for murdering the Son of God by their own demonically-influenced rationale was that Jesus "made Himself out to be the Son of God" (Jn. 19:7). But, not only was it not true that He was guilty of blasphemy in making Himself out to be the Son of God because He was indeed the Son of God, but God Himself personally had testified TWICE with His own Voice out of heaven that He was His "Beloved Son in whom I am well-pleased" (Mat. 3:17; 17:5) and commanded them to "LISTEN TO HIM!" Not only that, but the many mighty works of power Jesus performed testified irrefutably that He was the Son of God and God the Son, and He told them to believe on account of those works they had witnessed (Jn. 14:11). Indeed, when John the Baptist sent two of his disciples to Jesus to ask Him to verify with His own lips if He was the long-awaited Messiah, Jesus' response was to tell

John about the miracles He had been performing all around the region:

> Summoning two of his disciples, John sent them to the Lord, saying, "Are You the Expected One, or do we look for someone else?" When the men came to Him, they said, "John the Baptist has sent us to You, to ask, 'Are You the Expected One, or do we look for someone else?'" At that very time He cured many people of diseases and afflictions and evil spirits; and He gave sight to many who were blind. And He answered and said to them, "Go and report to John what you have seen and heard: the BLIND RECEIVE SIGHT, the lame walk, the lepers are cleansed, and the deaf hear, the dead are raised up, the POOR HAVE THE GOSPEL PREACHED TO THEM. (Lk. 7:19-22)

The Cause of the Great Persecution of the Early Church

And what was this great persecution of believers that occurred after the death of Stephen all about? It was all about that people were following the Name, the cause, the purposes of the Lord Jesus Christ, and because these people had received of that great outpouring, that original outpouring of the Holy Spirit on the Day of Pentecost.

What many commentators and expositors concerning this matter of the great persecution of the Early Church fail to recognize is the fact that all this demonically-inspired persecution was all because of what happened on the Day of Pentecost, when the Holy Ghost was poured out upon those 120 believers, and then 120 multiplied themselves, so to speak, into 3,000 more. And there were 3,120 on one day who had received of this power of the Holy Spirit, when they received the promise of the Father. They too received the power of God in their lives, and began to speak in other tongues, and were filled with ecstatic, overflowing, exceedingly great joy—joy unspeakable, and full of glory!

And religion—religious spirits, religious people, people filled with religious spirits—hate it when people express great joy that happens when you receive the Baptism in the Holy Spirit, a joy that is unexplainable, a joy that is uncontainable, a joy that is unstoppable, a joy that is indomitable! The one thing that religious spirits seek to do, is to make people dour, sour, unhappy, and sad, as they wallow in the muck and the mire of death's sorrow, mourning, and unbelief, languishing year after year in the inertia of dead ritualism and religiosity.

He whom the Son sets free, is free indeed (Jn. 8:36)! And religious spirits absolutely despise, abhor, and hate people who have been set free from the bondages of Satan and his kingdom. Religious spirits make people hate and loathe people who are walking in the liberty that only Jesus can provide. It is a demonic jealousy that takes hold of them, because they are not experiencing this same elation—joy unspeakable and full of glory (1 Pet. 1:8)—and that "peace which passeth all understanding" (Plp. 4:7)!

Religion only brings you back under bondage. And this great apostle, Paul, later said to the Galatian Church, "It was for freedom that Christ set us free; therefore keep standing firm (i.e., in that liberty, or in that freedom), and do not be subject again to a yoke of slavery" (Gal. 5:1). He was telling them: don't let anybody or anything bring you back under the bondage that you were under before you came to Christ.

My friends, Satan hates the Baptism in the Holy Spirit! And that's why all throughout history, whenever there's been a great move of God, and there's been a renewal of the Baptism in the Holy Spirit, and people were being filled with the Holy Spirit, and received the ecstatic joy that accompanies the great gift of *tongues* and all of the other manifestations of the Spirit that come with the Baptism in the Holy Spirit (nine of them in all), Satan has mounted a vicious, no-holds-barred counterattack against those believers who were the recipients of the outpouring of the Spirit perpetrated through diabolical religious agents, possessed by demons of rage and murder.

What else would make those who composed the body of the Sanhedrin Council want to murder a man (Stephen)?

Was he a child molester? No! Was he a rapist? No! Was he a thief? No! Was he a murderer? No! He merely was performing great works and signs and wonders among the people as a result of having been baptized in the Holy Ghost.

What else would make religious people so enraged, but evil spirits? It is evil spirits that caused the Apostle Paul (then, Saul) to be in hearty agreement with putting to death this great martyr, Stephen. It was evil spirits that made Saul think to himself that he "had to do many things hostile to the name of Jesus." This was not *natural*. This was not *normal*. But rather this was *supernatural*. This was *paranormal*.

What else but religious spirits would make this man himself say, "As I punished them often in the synagogues, I tried to force them to blaspheme, and being furiously enraged at them, I kept pursuing them, even to foreign cities." What in this world would make him be furiously enraged at these Christians? Had they wronged him in any way? No! Had they stolen anything from him, or mistreated him? No! But rather it was the murderous religious spirit that was at work in him at that time that made him *furiously enraged* at those who were belonging to The Way.

Now there are many listening or reading right now, and you, friend, have been going to church, you may even be a preacher, and you have been furiously enraged at those who have been baptized in the Holy Ghost, those who name themselves among the Pentecostal way, or the Charismatic way, or perhaps are a part of some Neo-Pentecostal branch of the church, and you, sir, you, lady, also have been *furiously enraged* at such people. And you know yourself that whenever you think about it, you talk about it, you talk about those people, and make those charges, that there's some sort of fury that rises up within you that you can't even understand where it comes from.

Well, I'll tell you where it comes from, my friend: It comes from demonic religious spirits, the same spirits that caused Saul to be in hearty agreement with putting to death the martyr, Stephen. How can anybody possibly say they serve God, love God, and be in agreement with murdering a saint of God? And, yet, the Bible says that if you hate your brother—someone that is born-again, someone who has also been adopted into the family of God just as you have been—if you hate your brother, you are a murderer, and it says that we **know** that *no murderer* has eternal life abiding in him (1 Jn. 3:15)!

Call To Repentance of the Eternal Sin

Everyone listening to the sound of my voice or reading these words right now, you may be a Christian who has attended church for years and years, you may be a deacon in your church, or you might even be the preacher, but there is something in you that becomes agitated and even enraged by the mere discussion of this whole matter of the Baptism in the Holy Spirit—I guarantee you right now, and I know that I'm speaking under the inspiration of the Spirit of God at this very moment—that is not merely *you* that is so enraged, but rather it is a religious spirit! And you need to fall down on your knees before God *right now*, and beg Him to forgive you of your years of resistance to the Holy Spirit, before you cross the line of out-and-out blasphemy against the Holy Spirit, from which there is no return, and no hope of repentance, like Esau, who sought for it with tears (Heb. 12:17).

Jesus made it abundantly clear that blasphemy against the Holy Spirit is the unforgivable or unpardonable sin, which manifests in the form of religiosity that condemns and mocks the works and manifestations of the Holy Spirit, and attributes it to Beelzebub, or Satan. (Mk. 3:29).

Please listen to this lonely cry out of the wilderness today, repent *now*, while there is still time, and while there is still grace being extended to you by the God of all grace. This man named Saul tried to get these people belonging to The Way to blaspheme because he himself was filled with a spirit of blasphemy, an evil spirit of blasphemy that was working through him, trying to get other people to blaspheme against God. Friend, repent today, and ask God to forgive you of your ungodliness and being a resister of the Holy Spirit (Ac. 7:51).

Supernatural Demonic Persecution, Not Mere Flesh and Blood

Thus, it was not just flesh and blood that was bringing forth this great persecution against the Church, but rather it was inspired by Satan himself, for we war not against flesh and blood, but against the rulers, the powers, and the evil forces of wickedness at work in the Heavenly places (Eph.6:12). And Satan was enraged that the Holy Spirit had now come upon the Church, and empowered them with great power—Dunamis-Power! the power of God Himself—to plunder his kingdom and counter his power.

And truly the works that Jesus did, did these witnesses also begin to do, and even greater works than Jesus did, did they do. The Apostle John tells us that it was for this cause, for this reason, for this purpose, that Jesus was manifest—that He might destroy the works of the devil (1 Jn. 3:8). And that is precisely what was happening through these people that belonged to the Early Church—they were destroying the works of the devil by bringing forth healing, deliverance, and great works of power as a result of having been baptized in the Holy Spirit (cf., Ac. 2:43-47).

It was the religious evil spirits that caused this great persecution to rise up against the Church. And it was these evil religious spirits that caused Saul to breathe out threats and murder against the disciples of the Lord. And it was these same evil spirits, these religious evil spirits, that caused the Apostle Paul, in his own words, to think that he "had to do many things *hostile* to the name of Jesus of Nazareth" (Acts 26:9).

It is the same evil, sadistic, and self-righteous spirits that caused him to "lock up many of the saints in prison (verse 10), having received authority from the chief priest, but also when they were being put to death," he said, he "cast his vote against them." "And," he goes on to say, "as I *punished them* often in all the synagogues, I tried to force them to blaspheme; and **being furiously enraged at them**, I kept pursuing them even to foreign cities." Though it is shocking and offensive to the religious mind to hear such a thing, this man named Saul, a self-described "Hebrew of Hebrews; as to the Law, a Pharisee" (Plp. 3:5), without a shadow of a doubt, was himself *demonized* with a religious spirit of murder that caused him, in his own words, to be "furiously enraged" at these believers. And, in verse 2 of Chapter 9 of the book of Acts, he says that (when) "he found any belonging to The Way, both men and women, he (would) bring them *bound* to Jerusalem."

In the same manner, these legalistic religious people today that call themselves Christians, and claim to be operating in true Christianity, try to bring people under their religious bondage, and try to bring them *bound* also unto their churches and Sanhedrin councils, and keep them bound by their religious chains. The moment the neophyte believers get free in Jesus, these religionists—modern-day Pharisees, Sadducees, "wouldn't-sees," and "couldn't-sees"—try to bind them all up in their religiosity. This man Saul, by his own admission, was one of these. In fact, he was proud of his bona fides of being a Hebrew of Hebrews and Pharisee of Pharisees. And, yet the story goes on to show that there is even hope for the most murderous of Pharisees, for this is the story of a man named Saul, a self-appointed Jewish bounty hunter, who got knocked off his high horse on the way to arrest more of these blasphemous "Christians," and who eventually became the great bondservant of Jesus, the eminent Apostle Paul.

Continuing with the story in verse 3 of Chapter 9 of Acts, it says, "As he was traveling"—there are those listening to the sound of my voice and reading these words, and as they are continuing to travel on their own idolatrous, made-up, humanly contrived road of religiosity, they are about to have a divine encounter with the Truth—**Jesus**—also!

"...it happened that he was approaching Damascus, and

suddenly a light from heaven flashed around him" — and that light, we know, was the Light of the world, the Lord Jesus Christ Himself.

"And he fell to the ground...." Friend, you're too late to talk to me about people feigning it and faking it when they are in the presence of Jesus and they are knocked off of their high horse, or they fall to the ground. When you are in the presence of Jesus, you *will be* knocked to the ground, so to speak, one way or another. How could anyone not be!

Yes, the great Apostle Paul was "slain in the Spirit!" So all you preachers out there, and others who mock this matter of being slain in the Spirit, you are mocking the Apostle Paul, and his experience with the Lord Jesus Christ, as well as the experience of other disciples in the Bible, including the Apostles of the Lamb. They were *all* slain in the Spirit on the Day of Pentecost. And it says, the Apostle Peter, "taking his stand" — the reason he was taking his stand was because he wasn't standing previously, probably because he had been slain in the power of the Holy Spirit. And there are so many other examples in the Bible of people being slain in the Spirit and falling down in the presence of Almighty God, though time and space precludes us from going into that topic here in this context.

But, not only was the Apostle Paul slain in the Spirit when this experience happened on the road to Damascus, but he says in his account of this incident before King Agrippa and the Governor Festus, in Acts 26:14: "And when *we* had *all* fallen to the ground." So, it was not just Saul who was slain in the Spirit, but it was *all* of the men who were accompanying him, they too were slain in the Spirit, knocked off their horses, and knocked to the ground in the presence of the Lord Jesus Christ; more accurately, merely by the sound of His Voice!

I don't know what makes anybody think that if they are truly in the presence of the King of kings, the Lord of lords, the Sovereign God and Creator of the Universe, the God of all Glory, they would *not* be slain in the Spirit in His presence. I do not understand at all why this is a phenomenon that so many people have so much trouble with; except that it is religious spirits that is behind that rationale that being in His presence is no different than being in the presence of your spouse or neighbor, or a street person.

Who is it that you think this Jesus is that you say you serve? Do you think He's just a man? Do you think He's just like you, or just like me? This Jesus *is* the **Power of God**! He is the Word of God, the Creator of the Universe. He is the Authority of God. He is God Almighty. So, of course, when people are in His presence, they are going to be slain in the Spirit! Like those soldiers in the Garden of Gethsemane, who came to get Him, and Jesus went out to them, and asked, "Whom do you seek?" And they said, "Jesus of Nazareth." And when He said, "**I AM** He," they all fell back and were slain in the Spirit. *Because He is the Great I AM!* And, when He said, "**I AM** He," the very power of God came forth through His voice and knocked those mere mortal and carnal humans back and down on their backside, demonstrating who He really is (Jn. 18:1-9)!

And picking back up in Acts 9:4, it says, "And He fell to the ground, and heard a voice saying to him, 'Saul, Saul, why are you persecuting Me?' And he said, 'Who are you, *Lord*?'" I think it is very important that you notice this word "Lord"—he called Him "*Lord*." Though he did not know his name, he knew without any doubt that the Voice speaking to him was the Lord. And He said, "I am **Jesus** whom you are persecuting!"

Now you need to understand that when you are persecuting the saints of God, when you are mocking and ridiculing those who belong to The Way, those who have been saved by the power of God, have been adopted into the very family of God, because they have received of the Dunamis-Power of the Holy Spirit with manifest evidence testifying of that fact, you are not just persecuting *them*, you are persecuting *Jesus Himself*. Jesus so identifies with His Brethren, God's Children, that He takes persecution against them *personal*!

Jesus continued on speaking to Saul, in verse 6, it says:

"But get up and enter the city, and it will be told you what you must do. The men who traveled with him stood speechless, hearing the voice but seeing no one. Saul got up from the ground, and though his eyes were open...."

Listen to this phrase, "and though his eyes were open, *he could see nothing.*"

There are many reading and hearing these words right now that, though your eyes are open, *you can see nothing* of what God is trying to show you in the Spirit realm, because you do not have eyes to see, and you do not have ears to hear, because you are merely walking in fleshly Christianity, you are walking in intellectualism and intellectual Christianity, and you have not been baptized in the power of the Holy Ghost, you have not received that very thing that you've been mocking. And so, though your eyes are open, you really cannot see at all! Though in your spiritual delusion you think you see, there is no servant who is as blind, God says, as the servants of the Lord who think they see but yet they do not see—*they are blind* (Is. 42:19).

And if you can read the entirety of the Bible, and not see this matter of the Baptism in the Holy Spirit, and how real it is, and how true it is, friend, *you are blind*! I don't care what your place is in the church. I don't care how long you've been going to that or the church. *You are blind*! I don't care if you sing in the choir. I don't care if you're a deacon. I don't care if you're a Sunday School teacher. I don't care if you are the preacher. I don't care if you're the president or overseer of the denomination you're affiliated with. If you cannot see in the entirety of the Bible the truth, the reality, of the Baptism in the Holy Spirit, friend, *you are spiritually **blind***. I condemn you not for that, but I am just telling you, as a servant of the Lord, as a spokesman of the Lord, that *you are blind*, and you need to pray and beg God to send you an Ananias to come to lay hands on you that your eyes might be opened!

And, as the Apostle Paul was praying, Jesus spoke to a

certain disciple named Ananias, and Ananias came and laid his hands upon this man named Saul, in order that the scales might fall from his eyes, in order that he might see. Verse 8 continues on to say, "And leading him by the hand, they brought him into Damascus."

Beloved, if you do not see this matter, if you've not yet received the Baptism in the Holy Spirit, you need to allow somebody to lead you by the hand in your spiritual blindness, and bring you into Damascus, bring you into the place of the Truth of the Lord Jesus Christ, to be able to receive this wonderful promise of the Father called, "The Baptism in the Holy Spirit!"

The Apostle Paul himself received the Baptism in the Holy Spirit when Ananias laid his hands upon him (Acts 9:17). And though the text in that chapter of Acts does not explicitly mention that he spoke in tongues at that moment, we do *know* that he did indeed receive the gift of *tongues* with the Baptism of the Holy Spirit, because this man named Saul, who later became the Apostle Paul, and wrote two-thirds of the New Testament, he himself testified in First Corinthians 14:18, "I thank God, **I speak in tongues more than you all.**" He said, "I thank God, I speak in tongues more than you all."

Not only that, but in First Corinthians 14:5, he said, "Now I wish that *you all*," speaking of all believers, "I wish that you **all** spoke in *tongues*." And we know that this was written under the inspiration of the Holy Spirit, for it says in Second Timothy 3:16 that *every word* in this Bible is God-breathed, God-inspired. And so, we know that these words were not inspired by the Apostle Paul, but they were inspired by the Holy Spirit Himself. And so it is God Himself who is saying to us through the Apostle Paul, "Now I wish that you *all* spoke in tongues."

Thus, certainly this is undeniably, incontrovertibly the desire of God for *every* Born Again believer—that they speak in tongues, as a result of receiving the Baptism in the Holy Spirit!

The Damascus Road Vs. the Damascus Room Experiences of the Apostle Paul

Though I've been quoting from and commenting on the account of the Apostle Paul's experience, for what I'm going to discuss now, let's look at the entire account recorded in Acts 9:1-17:

> Now Saul, still breathing threats and murder against the disciples of the Lord, went to the high priest, and asked for letters from him to the synagogues at Damascus, so that if he found any belonging to The Way, both men and women, he might bring them bound to Jerusalem. As he was traveling, it happened that he was approaching Damascus, and suddenly a light from heaven flashed around him; and he fell to the ground and heard a voice saying to him, "Saul, Saul, why are you persecuting Me?" And he said, "Who are You, Lord?" And He said, "I am Jesus whom you are persecuting, but get up and enter the city, and it will be told you what you *must* do." The men who traveled with him stood speechless, hearing the voice but seeing no one. Saul got up from the ground, and though his eyes were open, he could see nothing; and leading him by the hand, they brought him into Damascus. And he was three days without sight, and neither ate nor drank. Now there was a disciple at Damascus named Ananias; and the Lord said to him in a vision, "Ananias." And he said, "Here I am, Lord." And the Lord said to him, "Get up and go to the street called Straight, and inquire at the house of Judas for a man from Tarsus named Saul, for he is praying, and he has seen in a vision a man named Ananias come in and lay his hands on him, so that he might regain his sight." But Ananias answered, "Lord, I have heard from many about this man, how much harm he did to Your saints at Jerusalem; and here he has authority from the chief priests to bind all who call on Your name." But the Lord said to him, "Go, for he is a chosen instrument of Mine, to bear My name before the Gentiles and kings and the sons of Israel; for I will show him how much he must suffer for My name's sake." So Ananias departed and entered the house, and after laying his hands on him said, "Brother Saul, the Lord Jesus, who appeared to you on the road by which you were coming, has sent me

so that you may regain your sight and be filled with the Holy Spirit."

Now I think it's absolutely critical and in keeping with what we've already been discussing concerning the Holy Spirit, the Baptism in the Holy Spirit, and the two different, distinct and separate workings of the Holy Spirit—one in the regeneration or at salvation, and the other when a person is baptized in the Holy Spirit—for us to look at two things here in this last verse, verse 17. When Ananias entered the house and after he laid his hands on him according to what Jesus told them to do, he said to him, *"Brother Saul"*—he addressed him as being a *brother*. From this we can rightly deduce and know that at this point that Ananias came to the room in Damascus where Saul was staying—three days after the Damascus Road experience—Saul had already been saved.

Indeed, he had been saved during that Damascus Road experience, when the Lord Jesus appeared to him in the form of a light from heaven that flashed all around him, knocking him off his horse, as well as all of those who were accompanying him, at which time the Lord Jesus said to him, "Saul, Saul, why are you persecuting Me?" His response was (v. 5), "Who are you, *Lord*?" It is important that we notice, as mentioned before, that Paul *knew* at that moment that this was the *Lord* of lords, the King of kings, the Lord Almighty, God Almighty, the Maker and Ruler of the Universe. He had no doubt, when he met Jesus, that He was *Lord*, even though he was not sure at that moment what His name was. And then when he asked Him, "Who are you, Lord?" He responded and said, "I am Jesus, whom you are persecuting."

Now we see in verse 17 that Ananias was sent by Jesus Himself to lay hands upon this man named Saul, who later became the Apostle Paul. Ananias laid his lands upon this man, who was already a brother in the Lord, because he addressed him as, "Brother." And we know these words were inspired by the Holy Spirit, as they are recorded in the Bible (cf., 1 Tim. 3:16). This man named Saul was already a brother to Ananias, because he had been adopted into the family of God as a result of his encounter with the Lord Jesus Christ. And, being a Born Again believer, he was therefore a legitimate candidate for the Baptism in the Holy Spirit, and Jesus sent Ananias to lay his hands upon him, according to what he himself said, "that he might recover his sight," and that "he might be filled with the Holy Spirit."

Now I know that people teach that he was just being filled with the Holy Spirit at this moment in regeneration, but that cannot possibly be, because he was already calling him, "Brother," indicating he was already saved. Listen, you have an experience like Saul did on that Damascus Road where you see Jesus in the form of a light so bright that it blinds you, and you cannot see for three days, though your eyes are open yet you cannot see, you *will* get saved. And he *did* get saved. Thus, he was already saved.

So this was not the Holy Spirit coming to infill his dead human spirit, but rather this was the filling of the Holy Spirit that comes through the Baptism in the Holy Spirit—a supercharging, if you will, of the Holy Spirit—because this is the baptism that Jesus gives—the Baptism in the Holy Ghost and Fire, as John, the original Baptist, referred to it. What happens in this Baptism is similar to a pot of water that is totally full already, heating on a hot burner over a flame on a stove, and that water becomes supercharged by heat, and as the water begins to boil, the pot begins to be over-filled and it overflows and rolls over and out of the pot.

This is the kind of "filling" that happens with the Baptism in the Holy Spirit. That is what the Baptism in the Holy Spirit is like—it is an immersion of the Spirit-infused human spirit in the Waters of the Holy Spirit.

Paul Taught that All Believers Should Receive the Baptism in the Holy Spirit

The Apostle Paul himself received the Baptism in the Holy Spirit when Ananias laid his hands upon him. And though the text in this chapter of Acts does not explicitly state that he spoke in tongues at that moment, we do know, as indicated previously, that the Apostle Paul did indeed receive the gift of *tongues* with the Baptism of the Holy Spirit because he says in First Corinthians 14:18, "I thank God, I speak in tongues more than you all." "I speak in tongues," he said; "I thank God, I speak in tongues *more than you all.*" And then, in First Corinthians 14:5, he also says that it was his desire, his wish, that **all** Christians and everyone at Corinth would speak in tongues.

But, we know that is also the desire of the Holy Spirit, who inspired these words, for they are His words, not just the words of a man, not just the words of the Apostle Paul. According to Second Timothy 3:16, these words are inspired by the Holy Spirit Himself—"God-breathed," the original language states. He says, "Now I wish that you **all** spoke in tongues," speaking to *every* Born Again believer that has ever lived, from then until now and until Jesus returns. And then we can also ascertain from the Apostle Paul's teaching that is recorded in his many letters, or Epistles, in the New Testament, that he spoke and taught about this gift of the Baptism in the Holy Spirit and the gift of *tongues* that comes with it.

In his first letter to the Corinthian Church, the Apostle Paul highly commended the Corinthian Church for "not lacking in any gift." In First Corinthians 1:4-7, it says, "And I thank my God always concerning you, for the grace of God which was given you in Christ Jesus." Notice this word "grace," which in the Greek is the word *charis*, which is the same word for the word *gifts*. Grace and gifts—the word *charis* can be interpreted as both gifts and grace. He continues in verse 5:

> ...that in everything you were enriched in Him, in all speech and all knowledge, even as the testimony concerning Christ was confirmed in you, so that you are not lacking in any gift, awaiting eagerly the revelation of our Lord Jesus Christ.

And, of course, in this same Book, he goes on in Chapters 12 and 14 to talk about the Manifestation Gifts of the

Spirit (which we'll examine in Chapter Twelve), among other sets of gifts, each emanating from different members of the Godhead. In other words, he was saying to them that although there were some problems, which he would be addressing in his letter later, these Corinthians were nonetheless to be commended for the fact that they were operating in all of the gifts that are bestowed by the Members of the Godhead, which include those bestowed by the Holy Spirit, which are "the manifestations of the Spirit given for the common good"—nine of them in all, which he later enumerated in the Eleventh Chapter of the same book, his first letter to the Corinthians. The fact that the members of the Corinthian Church were not lacking in any gifts certainly is a testament of the ministry of the Apostle Paul, and demonstrates that the Baptism of the Holy Spirit was a central element of the Gospel he preached.

As we can see, not only here with the Corinthians, but also in his first meeting with the Ephesian believers (Acts 19), which we will examine in a later chapter, Paul always taught believers that once they had become believers and had thereby received of the regenerative working of the Holy Spirit, they were to also receive the Baptism in Holy Spirit, and thereby be imbued with the *dunamis*-power of God, in order to be effective witnesses of the risen Christ. In fact, it is incontrovertible that no New Testament writer conveyed more revelation and understanding concerning the Baptism of the Holy Spirit and the gifts of the Spirit that imbue true believers through the Baptism in the Holy Spirit than the Apostle Paul. One of the revelations he reveals is that praying in the Spirit primarily entails praying in *tongues*, because he says in the same letter to the Corinthians:

> "For, if I pray in a tongue, my spirit prays, but my mind is unfruitful. What is the outcome then? I will pray with the Spirit, and I will pray what the mind also. I will sing with the Spirit, and I will sing with the mind also." (1 Cor. 14:14-15).

Then, in his letter to the Roman believers, Paul gives us remarkable insight into how the Holy Spirit, who Jesus called, "The Helper"—the *paracletos* (Gr.), the One who stands alongside to help—takes hold with us when we pray in the Spirit, that is, in *tongues* in particular, and helps us with our weakness—and he explicitly and specifically identifies our weakness as being that we in ourselves do not know *how* to pray *as we should*, though we know we *need* to pray. But, the Holy Spirit, he says, takes hold together with us when we initiate prayer in the Spirit, and stands in the gap on behalf of—that is the meaning of the Greek word translated *intercede*—the person or situation we are praying about, and intercedes for us with groanings in the Spirit realm that are too deep for human words, but with the help of the Holy Spirit, He who searches the heart, knows what the mind of the Spirit is.

Thus, when we intercede in tongues, we actually engage in intercessory prayer for the saint or person that is in perfect accord, or agreement, with the will of God for whomever we are praying. This is all found in Romans 8:26-27, where it says:

> And in the same way the Spirit helps our **weakness; for we do not know how to pray as we should**, but **the Spirit Himself intercedes for us** with groanings too deep for words; and He who searches the hearts knows what the mind of the Spirit is, because he intercedes for the saints according to the will of God.

All of this is what the Spirit revealed to the Apostle Paul concerning the workings of the Holy Spirit. This is what he himself practiced in his personal life, and it is also what he taught the churches to which he ministered.

And so we can know without a shadow of a doubt from all of this that the great Apostle Paul himself received the Baptism in the Holy Spirit with the evidence of speaking with unknown *tongues*. Moreover, since God is no respecter of persons, it is His desire that *every* believer receive of the Baptism in the Holy Spirit with the evidence of speaking with unknown tongues.

Chapter Eight
The Samaritan Example

Now in this segment of teaching, we will continue our discussion regarding the Biblical, initial evidence that someone has received the Baptism in the Holy Spirit, which is the gift of *tongues*, that is, a supernatural enablement to speak in languages that the speaker has never learned. This is referred to in the Bible as *unknown tongues*. It is called *unknown tongues*, again, because the languages are unknown to the speaker.

Now the incident that we want to examine during this segment of teaching is that of the city of Samaria. We find this story in the Book of Acts, Chapter 8, verse 5:

> Philip went down to the city of Samaria and began proclaiming Christ to them. The crowds with one accord were giving attention to what was said by Philip, as they heard and saw the signs which he was performing. For in the case of many who had unclean spirits, they were coming out of them shouting with a loud voice; and many who had been paralyzed and lame were healed. So there was much rejoicing in that city. Now there was a man named Simon, who formerly was practicing magic in the city and astonishing the people of Samaria, claiming to be someone great; and they all, from smallest to greatest, were giving attention to him, saying, "This man is what is called the Great Power of God." And they were giving him attention because he had for a long time astonished them with his magic arts. But when they believed Philip preaching the good news about the kingdom of God and the name of Jesus Christ, they were being baptized, men and women alike. Even Simon himself believed; and after being baptized, he continued on with Philip, and as he observed signs and great

miracles taking place, he was constantly amazed. Now when the apostles in Jerusalem heard that Samaria had received the word of God, they sent them Peter and John, who came down and prayed for them that they might receive the Holy Spirit. For He had not yet fallen upon any of them; they had simply been baptized in the name of the Lord Jesus. Then they began laying their hands on them, and they were receiving the Holy Spirit. Now when Simon saw that the Spirit was bestowed through the laying on of the apostles' hands, he offered them money, saying, "Give this authority to me as well, so that everyone on whom I lay my hands may receive the Holy Spirit." But Peter said to him, "May your silver perish with you, because you thought you could obtain the gift of God with money! You have no part or portion in this matter, for your heart is not right before God."

Now it's important, as we examine this story, to remember that Philip was one of the early disciples who had himself received of the Baptism in the Holy Spirit. And it clearly says, in verse 12, that these people, *"believed* Philip (when he was) preaching the good news about the kingdom of God, and the Name of Jesus Christ." They became *believers* in Jesus Christ, and, indeed, they all were baptized in water, as a sign of identifying with Christ. And it says, "Even Simon himself (this magician) *believed*, and (was also) *baptized*, and continued on (traveling) with Philip, as he observed the signs and great miracles that were taking place" through the ministry of Philip, and he was constantly amazed.

Even though these great signs were taking place through the ministry of Philip, nevertheless, the Holy Spirit "had not yet fallen upon" the believers through the anointing or the ministry of Philip the *evangelist*. And so, "when the *apostles* at Jerusalem heard that Samaria had received the word of God, they sent to them Peter and John," who were both *apostles*, whereas, Philip was an *evangelist* (Ac.21:8); he was not an *apostle*. The Church sent the *apostles* down to pray for these believers "that they might receive the Holy Spirit," it tells us in verse 15.

And, then in verse 17, it tells us that when these *apostles*, Peter and John, began to lay their hands upon these believers they then "were receiving the Holy Spirit." Now some critics of this matter of the initial evidence of the Baptism of the Holy Spirit being *tongues*, will take issue here, and use this particular incident, as a pretext, pointing out that in this case, it does not explicitly say that these disciples spoke in tongues when the Holy Spirit came upon them.

However, in verse 18, it says, "Now when Simon *saw* that the Spirit was bestowed through the laying on of the apostles' hands, he offered them money." So, while it does not explicitly say, that these individuals spoke in tongues after receiving the Baptism in the Holy Spirit, yet implicit in what this verse states is evidence that they indeed *did* speak in tongues, for how else would Simon *see* that the Spirit had been bestowed upon these believers, except that when hands were laid upon them they began to speak in languages which they did not know.

We know of a certainty that when it says he "SAW that the Spirit was bestowed through the laying on of the apostles' hands," it had to be talking about some outward evidence that Simon perceived with his physical senses that the people had been filled with the Holy Spirit, because he certainly didn't *see* the Holy Spirit, because He is a spirit-being who cannot be seen by the physical eye. Thus, it had to be some kind of supernatural manifestation that registered on his physical senses for him to have *seen* that these believers had received the Holy Ghost.

And, then, he specifically asked the apostles to give him this *authority*—*authority*, he called it—that everyone on whom he laid his hands would receive the Holy Spirit. Some mistakenly say that Simon was trying to buy the Holy Spirit, but that was not his interest. His interest was to have this authority so that he could then make money on offering to lay hands on people to receive the ability to speak in languages they had never learned. Sort of a short-cut to the modern Rosetta Stone® type language-learning products that would certainly surpass even the Pimsleur® method for language-learning.

Something certainly happened there that indicated to Simon that these believers also had received the Baptism in the Holy Spirit. And since evidence of speaking in tongues is the pattern that is explicitly stated everywhere else in the Bible, there is no reason, whatsoever, to believe that these believers did not also receive the gift of *tongues* when the Holy Spirit fell upon them. Rather, based on the pattern established with all the other incidences recorded in the Bible in which believers received the Baptism in the Holy Spirit with the initial evidence of tongues, it would be illogical to conclude that the evidence of tongues was *not* what Simon saw. And this conclusion would coincide with the words Peter used in his explanation of what was occurring on the Day of Pentecost in which he said, "Therefore having been exalted to the right hand of God, and having received from the Father the promise of the Holy Spirit, He has poured forth this which you both see *and hear* (Ac. 2:33).

Moreover, there is yet another somewhat obscure and essentially unknown issue embedded in this story relative to Peter's response to Simon's request that they give him this authority to lay hands on people to activate the gift of tongues in them. Examine carefully Peter's response:

> But Peter said to him, "May your silver perish with you, because you thought you could obtain the gift of God with money! You have no part or portion in this *matter*, for your heart is not right before God." (Ac. 8:20-21; NASB)

The Greek word translated "matter" in verse 21 is actually *logos* [1], one of the words rendered "word" in the New Testament, and the same root of the word translated "utterance" in Acts 2:4, where it says, "And they were all filled with the Holy Ghost, and began to speak with other tongues, as the Spirit gave them UTTERANCE." So when Peter rebuked Simon, saying, "Thou hast neither part nor lot in this *matter*," he was literally saying, "Thou hast neither part nor lot in this matter of supernatural UTTERANCE"—meaning, this matter of speaking with other tongues.

And, if Simon himself had not received the Baptism with the gift of tongues, then he could not impart the gift to others. As stated a number of times elsewhere in this volume, one cannot bestow unto others what he himself has not first received and thereby possessed. Or, in other words, one has to be the legitimate owner of something before he can legitimately give it to someone else. Jesus, for example, was legitimately the Baptizer in the Holy Ghost because He had first Himself received the Baptism in the Holy Ghost when He came to be baptized in water by John the Baptist at the Jordan River and the Spirit lit upon Him in the form of a Dove. Since He Himself was a recipient of the Baptism in the Holy Spirit, He was then able to impart it to others!

This matter is perhaps the most conclusive proof of all that these Samaritan believers spoke with other tongues when they were filled with the Holy Spirit.

And so we see from this example as well that *tongues* is the Biblical initial evidence that a believer has received the Baptism in the Holy Spirit.

Endnote:
[1] Strongs (G3056): logos; log'-os; From G3004; something said (including the thought); by implication a topic (subject of discourse), also reasoning (the mental faculty) or motive; by extension a computation; specifically (with the article in John) the Divine Expression (that is, Christ): - account, cause, communication, X concerning, doctrine, fame, X have to do, intent, matter, mouth, preaching, question, reason, + reckon, remove, say (-ing), shew, X speaker, speech, talk, thing, + none of these things move me, tidings, treatise, utterance, word, work.

Chapter Nine
The Gentile Example

In this chapter, we continue our examination of Biblical examples that demonstrate that the initial evidence someone has received the Baptism in the Holy Spirit is endowment with the gift of *tongues*; which is a supernatural enablement to speak in languages that the speaker has never learned, and is therefore often referred to in the Bible as *unknown* tongues. It is called, *unknown tongues*, again, because the language is unknown to the speaker.

In every case in the Bible in which believers were reported to have received the Baptism in the Holy Spirit, the initial evidence, or indicator, or sign of their having received it was that they spoke in *tongues*. Moreover, there is no instance recorded in the Bible in which believers received the Baptism in the Holy Spirit without receiving and manifesting the gift of *tongues* as the initial evidence of having received it. By no means are *tongues* the *only* sign of the Baptism in the Holy Spirit, but they are the *initial* sign. Indeed, the Apostle Paul tells us in First Corinthians 14:22 that *"tongues* are for a sign to unbelievers," meaning an indicator testifying of the supernatural power of God being manifest in and through a Spirit-baptized believer.

For additional proof of this incontrovertible fact, in this segment, the example we examine is that of Cornelius' house—who were Gentiles—receiving the Baptism in the Holy Spirit. Our text for this example is found in Acts 10. And we read in verses 1 and 2:

> Now there was a certain man at Caesarea named Cornelius, a centurion of what was called the Italian cohort, a devout man, and one who feared God with all

his household, and gave many alms to the Jewish people, and prayed to God continually.

So we see that this man named Cornelius was a devout, God-fearing man who had taught his whole family to fear God, and that he was continuously giving alms to the Jewish people (that he was actually giving to *God*), and that he prayed continually to God. And we are going to see how these acts of faithfulness toward God resulted in him receiving the favor of God. But really, to understand this scenario, we must understand that it actually began with Jesus' command to the Early Church, especially to the apostles, "to go into all the world and preach the Gospel to all creation," as we see in Mark 16:15 and the verses following, "He who has believed"—he is saying, *everyone* who believes, *anyone* who believes—"and has been baptized shall be saved; but he who has disbelieved shall be condemned." In other words, Jesus is telling the apostles that this is a "whosoever Gospel"—a Gospel of Good News—that whosoever believes upon the Lord Jesus Christ shall be saved, and this is without regard to ethnicity or nationality.

In Matthew 28:19, we see Jesus' final charge to the original apostles, in which He says, "Make disciples of **all** of the *nations*," and that Greek word there for *nations* is the word *ethnos*, which means all *ethnicities*, or all peoples of all nations.

In Luke 24:47, we see that Jesus again gave the charge to preach "repentance for the forgiveness of sins," and that it should be proclaimed in Christ's name to *all* nations, to *all* ethnicities, to *all* ethnos, to *all* peoples. And then, in Acts 1:4 and verses following, we see that Jesus:

> gathered together the apostles, and He commanded them not to leave Jerusalem, but to wait for what the Father had promised, "Which," He said, "You heard of from Me; for John baptized with water, but you shall be baptized with the Holy Spirit not many days from now."

And, as I pointed out previously, this was *after* what occurred on the evening of Resurrection Sunday in the Upper Room, when these apostles and all of the brethren assembled together there, received for the first time the *infusion* of the Holy Spirit in *regeneration*. And they were born again at that time, on Resurrection Evening. And so, Jesus is not speaking here about the Holy Spirit coming in *regeneration*, but rather He is talking about the *Baptism* in the Holy Spirit. And, in verse 8, Jesus says, "But you shall receive power when the Holy Spirit has come upon you and you shall be My witnesses both in Jerusalem and in Judea and Samaria and even to the remotest part of the earth."

And so, again, Jesus' charge to the Early Church was to preach the Gospel to *all* peoples, not just to the Jewish people, and not just within the nation of Israel, but to the remotest parts of the Earth. And the Gospel that He told them to preach was a Gospel that included the Baptism in the Holy Spirit. And this baptism was for *all* peoples, for *all* nations throughout the world.

Indeed, we see in Acts 2 that when the Spirit was indeed finally poured out upon the disciples on the Day of Pentecost, they *all* began to speak with unknown *tongues*, and the other people living in the area heard them praising God in every language spoken by every people-group, or ethnicity, known to the world at that time. It says in the account, beginning in verse five:

> Now there were Jews living in Jerusalem, devout men, **from every nation under heaven**. And when this sound occurred, and the crowd came together, they were bewildered, because each one of them was hearing them speak in his own language. And they were amazed and astonished saying, "Why, are not all of these who are speaking Galileans? And how is it that we each hear them in our own language to which we were born? Parthians, and Medes and Elamites, residents of Mesopotamia, Judea and Cappadocia, Pontus and Asia, Phrygia and Pamphylia, Egypt and the districts of Libya around Cyrene, and visitors from Rome, both Jews and Gentiles (original language), Cretans and Arabs—we hear them in our own tongues speaking of the mighty deeds of God." And they all continued in amazement and great perplexity, saying to one another, "What does this mean?"

And, of course, as we know, the Apostle Peter stood up later and began answering their questions, saying, *"This is that* of which the Prophet Joel spoke," and he goes on to say, "I will pour forth of My Spirit on *all* mankind." And so that means *all* peoples of *all* nations, *all* ethnicities who receive the true Gospel of the Lord Jesus Christ, receive the gospel of repentance for sins, and the Gospel that includes the Baptism in the Holy Spirit. Despite this charge which Jesus gave "to go into all the world and preach the Gospel to every creature and in every nation," the Early Church was reticent or slow to obey Jesus' command "to *go into all the world* and to preach the Gospel of Good News." Rather, they continued to stay in Jerusalem and direct the majority of their evangelizing to the Jewish people in and around that region.

It was because of this that the great persecution, which we saw in Acts 8, arose against the Church in Jerusalem, which according to verse 1, caused the early disciples to be scattered throughout the regions of Judea and Samaria; all of them, except *the apostle*s, that is. The apostles apparently remained in Jerusalem. But, many of the disciples were scattered out and forced out of Jerusalem, due to this great persecution that arose. And, as I have pointed out in previous portions, one of the main personalities in that persecution was a man named Saul, who later became the Apostle Paul.

Again, this great persecution was really all about our primary topic—the Baptism in the Holy Spirit. And we are told it was due to this great persecution that Philip, who is called, Philip *the evangelist* (Acts 21:8), actually went down to the city of Samaria and began to proclaim Christ to them.

With that as our background, we go then to Chapter 10 of Acts, which historians tell us probably occurred somewhere around the ninth or tenth year after the Day of Pentecost. And we see in the account, in verse 3, that "on one day, about the *ninth* hour of the day," it says (and I believe that is significant because the number *nine* represents the

Holy Spirit in the Bible), "About the ninth hour of the day, he (Cornelius) clearly saw in a vision an angel of God who had just come in to him, and said to him, Cornelius!'" And so the angel calls out his name, Cornelius responds, and says, "What is it, Lord?" He knows the angel is sent of God, and he begins to speak to the Lord Jesus Christ, and he asks Him, "What is it, Lord?" The angel said, "Your prayers and alms have ascended as a memorial before God." So, we see, in this story the Divine response to Cornelius' continuous prayers and alms giving, which is that he and his whole household are saved, and they received this tremendous promise of the Father, the Baptism in the Holy Spirit, though they are Gentiles. But, again, this is according to what Jesus had said in the first place.

Then, the angel tells Cornelius to dispatch some men to Joppa to summon a man named Simon Peter, who is staying there in Joppa with another man also named Simon, Simon the Tanner. Cornelius obeys the angel, and sends the men. The next day, while the men were on their way to Joppa, at around noon, Peter went up on the housetop to pray. At that time, we are told in verse 10, "And he became hungry, and was desiring to eat," this no doubt, prepared him for what was about to occur.

Then, the Bible says he fell into a trance, and while he was in that trance, he had a vision that repeated itself three times, indicating that this was certainly something that was from God. And, while he was under this trance—

> he beheld the sky opened up, and a certain object like a great sheet coming down, lowered by four corners to the ground, and there were in it all kinds of four-footed animals and crawling creatures of the earth and birds of the air. And a voice came to him (saying), "Arise, Peter, kill and eat!" But Peter said, "By no means, Lord, for I have never eaten anything unholy and unclean" (for these were all things that were banned under the Old Testament Laws to the Jews). And again a voice came to him a second time (saying), "What God has cleansed, no longer consider unholy." And this happened three times, and immediately the object was taken up into the sky.

And verses 17 and following say:

> Now while Peter was greatly perplexed in mind as to what the vision which he had seen might be, behold, the men who had been sent by Cornelius, having asked directions for Simon's house, appeared at the gate; and calling out, they were asking whether Simon, who was also called Peter, was staying there. And while Peter was reflecting on the vision, the Spirit said to him, "Behold, three men are looking for you. But arise, go downstairs, and accompany them without misgivings, for I have sent them Myself."

Peter goes down, he talks to the men, telling them he is the one they are looking for and asking the reason they have come to summon him, which they explained to him, and Peter invited them in to stay for the night. And then on the next day, they depart to go to Cornelius' house. When they arrive at Cornelius' house and Cornelius meets Peter, he falls on his face to worship him, but Peter raises him up, telling him to stand up, that he is merely a man like him also. They go inside where there is a crowd of many people assembled, and Peter says to the crowd assembled:

> "You yourselves know how unlawful it is for a man who is a Jew to associate with a foreigner or to visit him; and yet God has shown me that I should not call any man unholy or unclean. That is why I came without even raising any objection when I was sent for. And so I ask for what reason you have sent for me." (Ac. 10:28-29)

And, then, Cornelius tells Peter the story of how the angel appeared to him and what he told him, and that he told him to send for this man called Peter. And, then, he says to Peter, "Now then, we are all here present before God to hear all that you have been commanded by the Lord." Beginning in verse 34, Peter begins to speak to them, and says:

> "I most certainly understand now that God is not one to show partiality, but in every nation, the man who fears Him and does what is right, is welcome to Him. The word which He sent to the sons of Israel, preaching peace through Jesus Christ (He is Lord of all)—you yourselves know the thing which took place throughout all Judea,

The Gentile Example   107

starting from Galilee, after the baptism which John proclaimed. You know of Jesus of Nazareth, how God anointed Him with the Holy Spirit and with power, and how He went about doing good, and healing all who were oppressed by the devil; for God was with Him. And we are witnesses of all the things He did both in the land of the Jews and in Jerusalem. And they also put Him to death by hanging Him on a cross. God raised Him up on the third day, and granted that He should become visible, not to all the people, but to the witnesses who were chosen beforehand by God, that is, to us, who ate and drank with Him after He arose from the dead. And He ordered us to preach to the people, and solemnly to testify that this is the One who has been appointed by God as a Judge of the living in the dead. Of Him all the prophets bear witness that through His name everyone who believes in Him receives forgiveness of sins. While Peter was still speaking these words, **the Holy Spirit fell *upon* all those who were listening to the message**. And all the circumcised believers who had come with Peter were amazed, because **the gift of the Holy Spirit had been poured out upon the Gentiles also**.

And what was this gift? This was that gift, that promise, which Jesus talked about, "You shall receive *power* after that the *Holy Ghost* has come upon you." For it says in verse 46, "For they were hearing them speaking with tongues and exalting God."

And so we see that the Holy Spirit fell upon these individuals, and the way that those who had been baptized also in the Holy Spirit who accompanied Peter knew that these Gentile believers had received the Baptism in the Holy Spirit as well was because they were hearing them speaking with tongues and exalting God. Once again demonstrating conclusively that the initial evidence that someone has received the Baptism in the Holy Spirit is the endowment of the gift of *tongues*, which is a supernatural enablement to speak in languages that the speaker has never learned.

Chapter 10
The Ephesian Example

We continue, in this segment of teaching, our examination of Biblical examples that demonstrate that the initial evidence someone has received the Baptism in the Holy Spirit is endowment with the gift of *tongues*. The example we examine in this segment, is that of the Ephesian believers, for which our text is Acts 19:1-7:

> It happened that while Apollo was at Corinth, Paul passed through the upper country, and came to Ephesus, and found some disciples. And he said to them, "Did you receive the Holy Spirit when ("since"; KJV) you believed?" And they said to him, **"No, we have not even heard whether there is a Holy Spirit."** And he said, "Into what then were you baptized?" And they said, "Into John's baptism." Paul said, "John baptized with the baptism of repentance, telling the people to believe in Him who was coming after him, that is, in Jesus." And when they heard this, they were baptized in the Name of the Lord Jesus. **And when Paul had laid his hands upon them, the Holy Spirit came on them, and they began speaking with *tongues* and prophesying.** And there were in all about twelve men.

Now I like to refer to this incident of these twelve disciples of the Lord at Ephesus as *The First Baptist Church at Ephesus*. And there's good cause for that. Because these believers indicated, upon the Apostle Paul's questioning, that they were actually followers of John the Baptist, the original Baptist, John **the Baptist**, who were true believers in the Lord Jesus Christ, who have indeed partaken of that baptism of John, which is a baptism of repentance for the forgiveness of sins. In fact, that is what the Apostle Paul told these Baptists in this text we are looking at. In verse 4, he said, "John baptized with the baptism of repentance." But notice what he says after that: "telling the people to believe in Him who was coming after him, that is, in Jesus." And, John the Baptist's testimony concerning Jesus, as found in Matthew 3:11, was:

> "As for me, I baptize you in water *for repentance*. But He who is coming after me is mightier than I, and I am not fit to remove His sandals; **He Himself will baptize you with the Holy Spirit and fire**." (NASB)

And so John was saying that the baptism that he initiated the people in was a baptism done by men, to recognize that they have received the Lord Jesus Christ. It is a symbol of salvation. The baptism in water does not save you, but it is a symbol that you are already saved, and that you have confessed the Lord Jesus Christ. In water baptism, as you go down under the water, what you are saying is: the old man is going down under this water, and is dying, and what is coming up is this new creature in Christ Jesus; the old things have passed away, and, behold, new things have come (cf., 2 Cor. 5:17).

This is a baptism of repentance—a baptism in which you have changed your mind concerning the old life, and now you have turned, and set your face like a flint toward the Kingdom of God—no longer will you live for Satan and his ideology, his thinking, his way, but now, you will live according to the word, will, and ways of God. It is a baptism of repentance, water baptism. But John always testified of the One who would come *after* him, saying that you needed to receive the baptism that *He* gives, which is a mightier baptism, because this is the baptism about which Jesus spoke, saying, "You shall receive **power** after that the Holy Ghost has come upon you."

That is why John said, "He would baptize you in the Holy Ghost and Fire." Fire, in the Bible, always symbolizes *the power of God*. In fact, in one place, the Bible says that "our God **IS** a consuming *fire*" (Heb. 12:29).

These disciples that the Apostle Paul found in Ephesus

were indeed disciples of the Lord Jesus Christ. Now, over the years, there has been a teaching propagated purporting that these twelve men here, who were called *disciples*, were not truly disciples of *Jesus*, but rather disciples of *John*. However, there are a number of reasons that that cannot possibly be the case. Chief among those is the fact that the Book of Acts is part of canonized Scripture; part of the sixty-six books that have now been canonized and we now call, *The Bible*, or Holy Writ, or Scripture, *all* of which, according to Second Timothy 3:16, is "God-inspired," or "God-breathed"—meaning that it was not just written by men, but it is actually from the Breath, or *Spirit*, of God. The word for *breath* in the Greek is the same word for *spirit*, which is *pneuma*, the word for which we get *pneumatic*, and it means *breath*, and also means *spirit*. So, this is talking about the very *breath* of God. **All** Scripture is *God-breathed*.

Then it goes on to say that it is "profitable for *teaching*," or the King James says, "for *doctrine*," which certainly flies directly in the face of that teaching which has also come forth saying that the Book of Acts cannot be used for doctrine, and therefore what it has to say about the Baptism in the Holy Spirit is thus negated. That is a convenient teaching for those who want to try to refute the truth of the Baptism in the Holy Spirit, but is nonetheless false.

In fact, Second Timothy 3:16 says, "*All* Scripture is given by inspiration of God, and is profitable for *doctrine*"— it specifically says for *"doctrine."* That word in the Greek is the word for *teaching*—"for reproof, for correction, for instruction in righteousness, that the man of God"—it is especially talking about the *man of God*—the man who would purport to be a minister of the Lord Jesus Christ, a prophet, someone speaking on behalf of God—may be perfect, thoroughly furnished unto *all good works* (KJV)." All Scripture is given to perfect and thoroughly furnish that individual, the minister, *unto all good works*. This word that is translated *furnished* in the King James is actually talking about *equipping*. So, in order to be properly equipped for battle, if you will, to be properly equipped, or outfitted, the man of God must himself be thoroughly immersed in and teach out of ***all** Scripture*, that is, *"the whole counsel of God"* (Ac. 20:27; KJV).

And so the Apostle Paul finds these *believers*. And we know these were truly *believers* in the Lord Jesus Christ. In fact, the Amplified Version actually explicitly says that, for it renders verse 2 this way, "And he asked them, 'Did you receive the Holy Spirit when you *believed*?'" And, then, parenthetically it says, "on Jesus as the Christ." And, of course, that would have to mean that, and that is another reason that they could not possibly be merely disciples of John, because he is talking about *when you believed,* and all of the thrust of the Gospel is about believing—not upon *John*, but upon *Jesus*, as Lord and Christ. In order for this passage of Scripture to say what some people are attempting to make it say, it would have to mean that these believers were believers in *John* as the Messiah, rather than the Lord Jesus Christ. But, we know that is ludicrous. The salient point is that these Ephesians were already Born Again, spirit-infused believers. They had received the working of the Holy Spirit in regeneration, when they believed upon the Lord Jesus Christ.

And to his question, "Did you receive the Holy Spirit **when you believed**?" (the King James Version says *"since* you believed") they responded, "No, we have not even heard whether there is a Holy Spirit." This sounds so similar to many of our modern-day Baptist brethren (and others), who, unfortunately, have not even heard that there is such a thing as the Holy Spirit and the Baptism in the Holy Spirit, or they've heard erroneous teaching regarding it.

And then, Paul asked them, "Into what then were you baptized?" They said, "Into John's baptism." And Paul responded, "John baptized with the baptism of *repentance*, telling the people to believe in Him who was coming after him, that is, Jesus Christ."

Then, look at their response to what the Apostle Paul told them, in verse 5, "When they heard this, they were baptized in the name of the Lord Jesus Christ." Let me add very strongly here that this does not in any way mean what some people try to make this to mean, those that are referred to as "Jesus Only" or "Oneness," or "Modalists." This is not what this is talking about when it says, "In the name of the Lord Jesus Christ." This term, "in the name of the Lord Jesus Christ" in the Greek actually means *on behalf of the Lord Jesus Christ,* or *for this cause of Jesus.* So it was *into Jesus* that they were baptized, contrasted to John's baptism of repentance. That's the true meaning of what it's saying here. It is not establishing "Jesus only" dogma, as certain groups allege.

Now it is not really all that important, and we must not get dogmatic about it, but what I believe concerning this verse is that they were actually really baptized in water, and they were baptized in the Name of the Lord Jesus Christ, because they were not instructed properly about the baptism of John in the first place. For the true baptism that John was preaching was a baptism to demonstrate identification with Jesus as the Messiah, to testify that the Lord Jesus Christ is the Savior, and that they had identified and "connected" with Him.

And so they were baptized, and then, in verse 6, it says, "And when Paul had laid his hands upon them, the Holy Spirit came *on* them"—not *in* them. He was already *in* them, because they were believers of the Lord Jesus Christ who had confessed Christ and thereby were saved (Rom. 10:9). And, if they were legitimate disciples of Christ, then they had already been *infused* with the Holy Spirit in *regeneration*. The Holy Spirit, indeed, was resident in these believers' human spirit. So, when the Apostle Paul laid his hands upon them, the Holy Spirit came *on* them, not *in* them, and they began speaking with tongues and prophesying, as it percolated forth out of their innermost-being.

So, once again, we see in the example of the Ephesian believers that true *initial* evidence that someone has received the Baptism in the Holy Spirit is that they begin to speak with other tongues with the Spirit supplying the substance or essence of the utterance.

Now before I leave this topic of the Ephesian believers, I want to share some thoughts relative to this small group of Ephesian believers that sheds some light on why they believed the way they did at this point from my dear friend Charles Carrin. I will share more about him and his remarkable ministry history as well as some more quotes from him in later chapters. What follows here to the end of this chapter is an excerpt from one of his recent newsletters.

The Bible's Example of a Powerless Pastor Who Preached a Powerless Gospel

The Book of Acts gives us a working model of a conscientious, godly pastor who preached a powerless gospel. Like many today, Apollos was the pastor of a small, struggling congregation. He was faithful, loved God, served the congregation, but was totally bereft of power. While he was away from his home at Ephesus, Paul came and found his church of 12 male disciples with wives and children. In spite of Apollos having excellent credentials for ministry, Paul immediately recognized powerlessness in the man's flock. Both Paul and Apollos were servants of God, both equally loved the church, and each possessed vast knowledge of Scripture. Even so, a major discrepancy existed between their ministries. Paul had power; Apollos did not. Paul preached the gospel of the Kingdom; Apollos obviously knew nothing about it.

In light of the Apostle Jude's exhortation to "contend earnestly for the faith which was once for all delivered to the saints," we see how Apollos—though innocent of any evil intent—had accepted a *partial* gospel and experienced *partial* results. The ministries of Paul and Apollos are a parallel of pastors and churches today. I emphasize the fact that Apollos was ignorant because he had never been taught—not because he had knowingly rejected the truth. In our day pastors fall into two groups: Those who have never been taught and are innocently ignorant of spiritual gifts, and those who willfully reject spiritual gifts. Carefully observe these seven facts which Scripture records about Apollos (Ac. 18:24-28):

1. He was a Jew.
2. An eloquent man.
3. Mighty in Scripture.
4. Instructed in the way of the Lord.
5. Fervent in spirit.
6. Taught accurately the things of the Lord.
7. But: He knew only the "baptism of John"—that is, he knew nothing about the Baptism in the Spirit. He had a *partial* gospel and a *partial* faith.

When Paul recognized spiritual-powerlessness in the Ephesians, he asked the all-revealing question, "Did you receive the Holy Spirit when you believed?"They responded, "We have not so much as heard whether there is a Holy Spirit." This tragic ignorance existed because Apollos knew only the "baptism of John." He knew nothing about the baptism in the Holy Spirit and had left his congregation in that same condition. Paul immediately instructed the Ephesians about the Holy Spirit's empowering and when he "laid hands on them, the Holy Spirit came upon them, and they spoke with tongues and prophesied." That event proved to be a cataclysmic change not only for Ephesus but for the rest of the Roman world.

Under Apollos' ministry, the church at Ephesus accomplished absolutely nothing to awaken the city. It demonstrated no Kingdom power, remained spiritually paralyzed, and except for the local Synagogue, its presence was virtually unknown. In that state, the congregation had no effective witness, made no impact on the people, was no threat to "powers, principalities, rulers of the darkness of this world," et cetera. Instead, the dark cloud of paganism gripped the land with unchallenged control. The Temple of Diana—or Artemas—already famous as the greatest of all Seven Wonders of the Ancient World, dominated the area. It was in the shadow of this formidable enemy that this miniscule church, ineffective and unknown, lay dormant.

That changed when Paul arrived (see, Ac. 19). When he came on the scene, Ephesus experienced a "Kingdom of

God" earthquake. Paul was not the power, but he was the instrument for the truth that produced the shaking. He merely provided the window through whom the power roared; Apollos and twelve other windows were already present in Ephesus but they had never been opened.

Chapter Eleven
The Early Church Example

In this segment of teaching, we continue our examination of Biblical examples that demonstrate that the initial evidence someone has received the Baptism in the Holy Spirit is endowment with the gift of *tongues*, which is a supernatural enablement to speak in languages that the speaker has never learned, and is therefore often referred to in the Bible as *unknown tongues*. Our primary focus in this chapter is the example of the believers of the Early Church and the churches in particular that the Apostle Paul ministered to.

Now, of course, we know that all of the New Testament believers of the Early Church were *tongue-talkers*. They were baptized in Holy Ghost, because the Bible says that on the Day of Pentecost all of those believers that were present that day in Jerusalem were baptized in the Holy Ghost. Then, the Apostle Peter stood up, preached unto those others that were there, who had not yet received the baptism, and on *one day* three thousand others, not only were saved, but they also received the Baptism in the Holy Ghost (because the Baptism in the Holy Ghost is a part of the Gospel that all the original apostles preached).

At the beginning in the Early Church, when what many now would call "revival" broke out in which people were being saved en masse, the Jerusalem-based leaders of the church would send apostles to lay hands on the new believers in order for them to receive the Baptism in the Holy Ghost. For some time, it appears, in the Early Church, it was primarily *apostles* who laid hands upon people to receive the Baptism in the Holy Spirit, as well as for healing and other miracles: "and many wonders and signs were taking place through the *apostles*. It's unclear why this was so, and there's been many theories about it since, but, despite the false theorizations of some still today who have erroneously concluded that the Baptism in the Holy Spirit can only be imparted through the laying on of hands by legitimate apostles, and under some of those theories that is more reason that the Baptism in the Holy Spirit and the gifts that come with it "ceased" following the death of the original Apostles of the Lamb, such theories are easily debunked by the fact that Ananias, who was identified by the Spirit as "a certain *disciple*" and was not one of the original Apostles of the Lamb (Ac. 9:10), is the person God chose to lay hands on Saul to receive his sight and the Baptism in the Holy Spirit (Ac. 9:17). Moreover, subsequent to receiving the Baptism in the Holy Spirit himself, Paul, who was an apostle, but not one of the original Apostles of the Lamb, laid hands on other believers to receive the Baptism, and when they received it, they too spoke in other tongues (Ac. 19:6). So, again, just those two examples shatter the theory that only apostles can lay hands on believers to receive the Holy Spirit baptism.

Technically speaking, we could also add to the examples that even the Gentile believers who had assembled at Cornelius' house to hear a message from Peter, because the account in Acts 10 actually specifically states that it was while Peter was still speaking that the Holy Spirit fell upon those present, without Peter laying hands on any of them and they all began speaking in other tongues, "For they were hearing them speaking with tongues and exalting God (Ac. 10:44-46)! And, tongues, nor the Baptism of the Holy Spirit, were even the topic of Peter's message. Peter never mentioned either in his sermon! The Holy Spirit didn't even wait till Peter finished his message and gave an altar call and had the musicians to come up and play before He fell upon these hungry and faith-filled believers! Many times if preachers will just keep it simple and brief and then shut up and let the Holy Ghost move, I believe, He would do the same thing today! Preachers often are so caught up in hearing themselves talk that they won't hush up long enough to allow the Holy Spirit to do what He wants to do!

One Requisite to Receive the Baptism in the Holy Spirit

Inherent in all this is one thing that's so important to understand: The one basic requirement for receiving the Baptism in the Holy Spirit is that you are a *believer* in the Lord Jesus Christ, and you've already been born again through the infilling of the Holy Spirit, the infusion of the Holy Spirit that comes into your dead human spirit at the moment of salvation when you accept Jesus Christ as your personal Lord and Savior. Why do I say that? Because in Ephesians, Chapter 2 it says that, "You were dead in your trespasses and sins." And so, before we come to the Lord Jesus Christ, and before we receive Him into our heart through the infusion of the Holy Spirit, our human spirit is dead, it exists, but it is dead spiritually. And, when we are saved, when we ask the Lord Jesus Christ to come into our lives, He comes in through the person of the Holy Spirit, and infuses us, infills us, with the very life, the nature, (Peter called it "the divine nature"), the life of God.

Some of what I've already stated elsewhere bears repeating as a backdrop for what I will discuss in this chapter and beyond. At the infilling of the Holy Spirit, we receive of the *fruit* of the Spirit; it's the *nature* of God that we receive at that time. But then, with the Baptism in the Holy Spirit, we receive the *power* of God, with which comes the *gifts* of the Spirit—the nine gifts of the Spirit enumerated in First Corinthians 12—what the Apostle Paul also called "the manifestations of the Spirit for the common good."

The First Baptist Church at Ephesus

In the previous segment of teaching, we saw one example of believers who the Apostle Paul ministered to, who received the Baptism in the Holy Spirit, which was the beginning of the church at Ephesus that began with twelve men there at Ephesus. The Apostle Paul came there and found these disciples, who were disciples of the Lord Jesus Christ, but who had come into that discipleship by way of the ministry of John the Baptist. And Paul, having found these believers, asked them, "What baptism were you baptized in?" And they said, "In the baptism of John." And the Apostle Paul explained to them that the baptism of John—water baptism—is a baptism of repentance for the forgiveness of sins, but John testified of One who would come after him, which was the Lord Jesus Christ, and they were to believe in *Him*. And so, they were then baptized again in water in the name of the Lord Jesus Christ, on behalf of the Lord Jesus Christ, baptized into Christ.

And then, the Apostle Paul laid his hands upon them, and they *all, all* twelve of these men, began to speak in other tongues, praising, worshiping, glorifying God, and they all prophesied as well, as a result of having received the Baptism in the Holy Ghost. And so, this original Baptist church, *The First Baptist Church of Ephesus*, went from being a Baptist church to being a Full Gospel Pentecostal church, because they were *all* filled with the Holy Ghost, as a result of receiving the Baptism in the Holy Ghost when Paul laid his hands upon them. As a result, these believers became what some refer to today as "Bapticostals."

The Corinthian Church

And then, in addition to the Ephesian Church, we also have the case of the Corinthian Church. In First Corinthians 1, the Apostle Paul says, "I thank God always concerning you for the *grace* (and that word *grace* in the Greek, is also the word for *gifts*) of God, which was given you in Christ Jesus; that in everything you were enriched in Him in all speech"—and that speech would include *tongues*, prophesying, and interpretation of tongues (tongues plus interpretation of tongues, equals prophecy, by the way, which we'll be talking about more in a later chapter)—"and all knowledge, even as the testimony concerning Christ was confirmed in you, so that you are *not lacking in any gift*." And the Apostle Paul in the same Book talks about "the manifestations of the *Spirit*"—the gifts of the Spirit, which are bestowed through that Member of the Godhead, the Third Member of the Godhead, the Holy *Spirit*.

It was in this letter to the Corinthian Church that the

Apostle Paul revealed the Manifestation Gifts of the Spirit. He began to speak to them about that, and so we have the text that is now canonized (made a part of Scripture). And in a part of that epistle, in the 12th and the 14th chapters, he speaks about these gifts of the Spirit, the Manifestation Gifts of the Spirit, what has been referred to as the *charismata* gifts. These are the gifts that are given by the Holy Spirit. They are the "manifestations of the Spirit for the common good." And one of those gifts is *tongues*. Just *one* of them is tongues, but there are in total *nine* gifts that come through the Baptism in the Holy Spirit, when a person receives the Baptism in the Holy Spirit.

And Jesus taught that these are manifestations of power—He said that "you shall receive power after that the Holy Ghost is come upon you!" So, these gifts are all *power manifestations*—manifestations of the power of God. And they are **all**, by the way, *super*natural; they are not *natural* gifts. These are *supernatural* gifts that emanate through the *supernatural* power of the Holy Spirit.

The Roman Church

There are numerous references in the Book of Romans, which the Apostle Paul also wrote—this is his letter to the Roman Church, an Epistle of the Apostle Paul to the Roman believers—to the power of the Holy Spirit and teaching that speaks, directly and indirectly, of the Baptism of the Holy Spirit, but especially Chapter 8, wherein he begins speaking about the role of the Holy Spirit in our lives. And what a glorious chapter this is—the Eighth Chapter of the Book of Romans. But space and time will only permit us to look at verse 26 and verses following, "So too, the Holy Spirit comes to our aid and bears us up in our weakness..." (AB).

There has been much teaching concerning this verse over the years, but much of it, unfortunately, does not capture the essence of what the Apostle Paul is truly saying here, for he goes on to say that our weakness is that we do not know what prayer to offer—reading from the Amplified Version: "We do not know what prayer to offer, nor how to offer it worthily as we ought." The New American Standard renders this verse this way, "And in the same way the Spirit also *helps* our weakness." Remember that Jesus called the Holy Spirit, "The Helper;" this is His name. So, certainly, one thing that the Body of Christ needs to understand is that, it is not blasphemous, it is not a bad thing, and the Holy Spirit is not insulted, when we ask Him to help us, for this truly is His name—"The Helper!"

What's in a name? Everything, my friend, everything! "And He (Jesus) was given a *name* which is above every name, that at the *name* of Jesus, every knee must bow, and every tongue confess that Jesus Christ is Lord, to the glory of God the Father" (Plp. 2:9-11). And, on and on and on, we could go, talking about those in the Bible who were given a new *name* by God; e.g., Abram, Jacob, Simon (Peter), Saul (Paul), et al.

The name that was given to the Holy Spirit is that name of "Helper," and he (Paul) says the weakness that we have is that we do not know how to pray as we should. We know we *should* pray, but the problem is we don't know *how* to pray *as we should*, in many various different situations. But the Spirit, it says, "*Himself* intercedes *for us* with groanings too deep for words." This is in reference to the gift of *tongues* and praying in *tongues*. The Apostle Paul made it very clear what praying in the Spirit is—in First Corinthians 14:14-15, he said, "For if I pray in a tongue, my *spirit* prays, but my mind is unfruitful. What then is the outcome? I **will** pray with the Spirit."

Notice it is a matter of our **will**. *Any* believer baptized in the Holy Spirit has the ability to pray in the Spirit *whenever* he/she *chooses* to exercise their prerogative to pray in the Spirit (contrary to the teaching of some Pentecostal denominations). "I"—I—who will? "I will,"—I! On the Day of Pentecost when they were filled with the Holy Ghost, the Bible says, "**They** were speaking in other tongues as the Spirit gave them utterance." In other words, the Holy Spirit gave them the substance of the utterance, but it was **they**—those believers—who were doing the speaking, operating their tongue, speaking forth the utterance given by the Spirit within their human spirit. And that's the way it is for us believers today—**I will** pray with the Spirit, and **I will** pray with the mind also. **I will** sing with the spirit, and **I will** sing with the mind also.

The Spirit-Baptism is for All believers and It's God's Desire For All Believers To Receive It

These examples I've cited in this and the previous chapters are just a few examples of those who were baptized in the Holy Ghost, especially those who were under the influence of the Apostle Paul's teaching. In every case, those who received the Baptism in the Holy Spirit, received the endowment, that special endowment, of speaking in other tongues, as an initial sign that they had received the power of the Holy Ghost through the Baptism in the Holy Ghost and Fire.

The preponderance of these examples we've discussed of believers receiving the gift of *tongues* through the Baptism in the Holy Spirit after the initial outpouring of the Spirit on the Day of Pentecost, conclusively demonstrate that this was not merely a phenomenon that occurred with the original outpouring for some parochial purpose, as some expositors would have us to believe. Rather, First Corinthians 14:5 makes it clear that God desires for *all believers* to speak in *tongues*. First Corinthians 14:14-15 makes it clear that all believers should pray and sing in the Spirit, that is to say, in *tongues* in their personal devotions and worship unto God.

Perfect Prayer

Moreover, First Corinthians 14:14 (below), where Paul instructs that when a believer prays in tongues, it is his spirit, infused with the Holy Spirit, that is praying, coupled with Romans 8:26-27 (below), makes it clear that praying in *tongues* allows and engages the Holy Spirit to take hold with the believer and begin to intercede with and for the believer, and the Holy Spirit always prays in *the perfect will of God*. And I ask you: who in his right mind would *not* want to pray in the perfect will of God? Especially since the

Apostle John revealed, in First John 5:14-15 (below), that when we "ask **ANYTHING** according to **His will**"—the will of God—we can have a confidence, an assurance, that God hears those petitions—because they are in accordance or agreement with His will—and if He hears them, then we can "know" that we have been granted—can count as our "present possession," the Amplified Bible says—what we have asked or petitioned Him for.

> For *if I pray in a tongue, my spirit prays*, but my mind is unfruitful. (1 Cor. 14:14)

> In the same way **the Spirit also helps** our weakness; for we do not know how to pray as we should, but the Spirit Himself intercedes for us with groanings too deep for words; and He who searches the hearts knows what the mind of the Spirit is, because He intercedes for the saints according to the will of God. (Rom. 8:26-27)

> This is the **confidence** which we have before Him, that, if we **ask anything according to His will**, *He hears us*. And if we know that He hears us in whatever we ask, *we know that we have the requests which we have asked from Him*. (1 Jn. 5:14-15)

Thus, what we learn from the confluence of the truth revealed in these Scriptures is that praying in tongues is praying in the perfect will of God, and praying in accordance with the perfect will of God is essentially perfect prayer, or what James called "fervent and effectual prayer that availeth much," (Jas. 5:16) because it is prayer that God always hears—because it is actually the Holy Spirit Himself, who IS God, who is doing the praying—and prayer that God hears is prayer that God always grants what has been petitioned from Him.

Our Predecessors in The Faith Were All Tongue-Talkers

In addition to that, it is also an incontrovertible fact that every New Testament Book was written by a *tongue-talker*—someone who had been baptized in the Holy Spirit and Fire, with the evidence of speaking in *tongues*. And that also would include *all* of the Apostles of the Lamb, The Twelve, meaning the original eleven, plus Matthias, who replaced

Judas, who hanged himself. *All* of the Apostles of the Lamb received the Baptism in the Holy Spirit on the Day of Pentecost, and *all* of them were filled with the Holy Ghost, and *all* of them spoke in other tongues.

So, clearly, this was the model given to *us* through the Early Church. And, certainly, that would put *us* in good company if we are among those who some like to call, *"tongue-talkers"*—the company, that is, of the Early Apostles and *all* of the New Testament believers, as well as *all* of those who wrote the New Testament Books of the Bible—they were all baptized in the Holy Spirit, and were *"tongue-talkers."*

As for me, I'm *thrilled* to be named among those individuals, those Early Church saints who spoke in tongues! But not only that, the Baptism in the Holy Spirit gives me the power that I *need* to be able to live the Christian life, to be able to resist the devil, and endure the onslaught of the devil, and to be able to do the works of Jesus that Jesus commanded *every* believer to do, saying, "Them that believe in Me, the works that I do shall they do also; and even greater works shall they do, for I go the Father" (Jn. 14:12).

Oh, friend, I urge you to receive that great Baptism in the Holy Spirit, in order that *you* might have the Dunamis-Power of God manifested in and through *your* life.

Chapter Twelve
The Charismata

> Now concerning spiritual gifts, brethren, I would not have you *ignorant*. (1 Cor 12:1).

Informed, Not Ignorant

As the above Scripture indicates, God desires for all believers to be INFORMED, NOT IGNORANT concerning the manifestation gifts of the Spirit, just as He desires for us to be informed about every other matter of the Spirit realm. Yet, there is perhaps more ignorance regarding this one matter than any other.

One of the remnants ostensibly of the Dark Ages in the Church that is still prevalent in many churches today is the ridiculous hypothesis that ignorance about spiritual matters perceived by some to be potentially erroneous is the best way to avoid deception. In other words, one should emulate the ostriches and bury his head in the sand so as to not even look upon anything which may be unorthodox or different than the traditional beliefs of the denomination or sect of which he is a part. Many denominational churches still teach that kind of childish and medieval-like behavior even for their adult church members pertaining to the matter of the Baptism in the Spirit and the Gifts of the Spirit, and some other related spiritual matters. Non-Pentecostal/Charismatic preachers and church leaders admonish their parishioners against becoming involved with groups espousing the Baptism and the Gifts with such foolish statements as "you better stay away from those 'tongue-talkers' and those 'holy-rollers' and those 'snake-handlers' lest some of that what they've got might get on you!" Again, the premise of their thinking, in sum, is that ignorance and avoidance of anything different than the traditional doctrines to which they ascribe is the way to prevent deception.

Nothing could be further from the Truth! Even the pagan Bereans had more spiritual sense than that, for when they heard the preaching by Paul of "another Way" than what they had known, they "received the word with great eagerness, *examining the Scriptures* daily to see whether these things were so" (Ac. 17:11). The only way to know whether a teaching is true or false is to examine it in the light of Scripture. The deception preventative prescribed by God's Word is to "Test and prove all things [until you can recognize] what is good; to that hold fast" (1 Thes. 5:21, A.B); and the only way we can *test and prove* any spiritual matter is by comparing it to Holy Scripture. If God's Word says it, then it is so. If it's in the Bible, it is truth!

Ignorance is not bliss, but stupid. Ignorance or avoidance of something is no safeguard against deception. God said His people are destroyed because of "LACK OF KNOWLEDGE" (Hos. 4:6). Lack of knowledge, or ignorance of the Truth, is what causes people to be destroyed. Knowledge itself never destroys—lack of knowledge does. It's not even knowledge of the untrue or the erroneous that destroys us, but rather lack of knowledge of the Truth!

Fear Not!

Believers must always receive truth by *faith*, and never *fear* it! It is fear of deception that we must reject. Without faith it is impossible to please God (Heb. 11:6); walking in fear rather than faith is not pleasing to God. The fact of the matter is that fear of *anything*, deception included, as the story of Job proves, will not only not *protect* us from it, but it will actually *produce* it. As Job said, "For the thing which I greatly feared is come upon me, and that which I was afraid of is come unto me" (Job 3:25). *Faith* in God and His published Word, the Bible, is our only true protection against evil and deception. That's why Jesus said to pray this way, "Our Father, which art in Heaven...*deliver us from evil*."

Fear is an evil *spirit* not given to us by God, but emanating from Satan (2 Tim. 1:7). Fear is the opposite of faith and produces the opposite results of faith. Faith is a real, effectual spiritual force of the Kingdom of God that produces those things that are desired (cf., Heb. 11:1). Fear, on the other hand, is a real spiritual force of the kingdom of Satan that produces the things that are not desired. Again, Job said, "The thing I have feared the most *has come upon me!*" *Sixty-three* times in the King James Version of the Bible, God issues the command, "FEAR NOT!"

Moreover, believers need not fear deceiving spirits—they have already overcome them (cf., 1 Jn. 4:1-6).

Love of and acceptance of the TRUTH is the only safeguard against DECEPTION and subjection to false signs and wonders (2 Thes. 2:7-12). It is those who refuse to become informed about and matured in the matter of spiritual gifts that will be more and more vulnerable to deception and false signs and wonders.

KNOWLEDGE OF THE TRUTH—knowing the Truth—is the only thing that will protect you from deception. Familiarity with the true spiritual gifts is the only thing that will protect us from accepting counterfeits. One of the best illustrations of that truth is U.S. Treasury agents, who handle thousands of genuine bills all day every day. They can spot a counterfeit in a second, just by the feel of it, because they handle so many millions of the *genuine*. Their elite training to readily detect fake bills is based preeminently on familiarization with the *genuine*, not concentrating on the *counterfeits*.

Supernatural gifts from God are the genuine—the real thing! Supernatural gifts of the Spirit originated with God, not the devil. Counterfeit signs and wonders do exist (2 Thes. 2:7-12)! Satan is the one who counterfeits the genuine gifts of God, not the other way around! The very existence of occult *counterfeit* signs and wonders is proof-positive of the existence of the *genuine* supernatural gifts of God. How do we detect, discern, or distinguish the counterfeit from the genuine? Not by ignorance of the genuine, but by as thorough a knowledge and familiarity with the genuine as possible! Like the U.S. Treasury agents and personnel, we become so knowledgeable of and familiar with the real that we can spot the bogus in a nanosecond!

The Charismata, or Spiritual Gifts, or Manifestation Gifts of the Spirit, however you refer to them, emanate from the Holy Spirit Himself, and are therefore part and parcel of God and His Kingdom and Divine Truth. Thus, we must not fear the Giver, The Holy Spirit, or the giftings He gives, or reject Him or them. To do so is insulting to God! Shying away from or resisting any aspect or element of the Kingdom of God because of fear of deception is itself deception and is precisely what the devil wants to cause believers to do, so that they will not be able to use the supernatural weapons of their warfare (2 Cor. 10:4) to defeat him and his kingdom. Neutralization is the closest thing to victory Satan can ever hope to achieve, but it's all he needs to achieve. To him, fear-driven <u>retreat</u> is tantamount to <u>defeat</u>!

A Trio of Gifts from the Trinity

In the Kingdom of the Triune-God, good things come in *threes*. Trinitarians espouse and expound the Truth that the Godhead consists of three *Persons*, as opposed to three *manifestations* as non-Trinitarian Oneness or Modalist Pentecostals contend. All Three Persons verily God, perfectly unified in essence and purpose, yet simultaneously separate and distinct—one God in Three Persons Trinitarians maintain.

"God so loved the world that He GAVE…" (Jn. 3:16). In this—the one most familiar and quoted of all Gospel verses—is reflected volumes more than what all the commentaries of Christian doctrine and theology have ever been able to suppose and propose. Add to it the fathomless precept of "the summing up of all things in Christ" (Eph. 1:10) and human ruminations of who God really is soar to such sublime heights so as to dizzy the most stolid and grounded of souls.

The preponderance of Scripture propounds over and over the phenomenal Truth that the One true Triune-God to whom traditional orthodox Christendom ascribes, avows, and serves is the Supreme Giver. It is undeniable and unavoidable that *giving* is a central attribute of the nature of God. He is "the God of all grace" (1 Pet. 5:10). He is so full of grace (charis, Gr.) [giftings], ever-lasting love and kindness, and mercy that endures to and throughout all generations (Psa. 100:5; et al.), that He simply cannot help Himself but to GIVE! He is a God of bountiful GIFTS and GIVING! When He gave us His only begotten Son, He GAVE all and the best He had to give. One of His names, El-shaddai, which means "the God who is MORE than enough," also demonstrates His nature of superfluous benevolence. When God gives, He gives in overflowing, abundant measure. It only follows then, as a brief aside, that anyone who purposes to emulate God and His attributes, in addition to all else, must also be a wildly generous and hilarious GIVER! (1 Cor. 9:7)

Now let's turn our attention to this trio of gifts bestowed unto believers by the Trinity. I will speak about each one only briefly, in that our main focus here in this chapter is the Manifestation Gifts of the Spirit.

> Now there are varieties of <u>GIFTS</u>, but the same <u>SPIRIT</u>. And there are varieties of <u>MINISTRIES</u>, but the same <u>LORD</u>. And there are varieties of <u>EFFECTS</u> (operations, KJV; energizings, lit. Gr.), but the same <u>GOD</u> who works all these things in all persons. (1 Cor. 12:46; NASB)

In these verses, the Spirit reveals through the Apostle Paul the truth that there are three distinct sets of supernatural spiritual giftings, each bestowed by and emanating from a different Member of the Godhead. To say it another way: The revelation of this passage is that each Person of the Godhead has a different set of gifts that emanate from that Member of the Trinity, which He bestows unto believers. Each set of gifting, in the system I espouse for these gifts, begins with the letter "M" in English; in order of their mention, they are: *Manifestation* Gifts, *Ministry* Gifts, and

Motivation Gifts. While the primary subject matter of this book is the Baptism in the Holy Spirit, it is almost irresponsible and negligent to address the matter without mentioning the Gifts of the Spirit or Charismata that inure to those who receive it, which I will do in this chapter only cursorily. I deal with them in greater depth in other books.

The Manifestation Gifts of the Spirit (Charismata)

"Now there are varieties of GIFTS, but the same SPIRIT." (1 Cor. 12:4)

The HOLY SPIRIT distributes MANIFESTATION GIFTS OF THE SPIRIT (cf., v. 7) (Charismata or Charismatic Gifts), which are supernatural empowerment bearing witnesses of the risen Christ (cf., Ac. 1:8), as He wills unto all Spirit-Baptized believers. This set of divine endowments is delineated in First Corinthians 12:7-11. They are NINE (the number of the Holy Spirit in Scripture) in number, and can be divided into three categories of three gifts each:

- REVELATION Gifts: word of wisdom, word of knowledge, discerning of spirits;
- POWER Gifts: healings, miracles, faith;
- PROPHETIC or VOCAL Gifts: unknown tongues, interpretation of tongues, prophecy.

The Apostle Paul's entire dissertation in chapters 12, 13, 14 of First Corinthians concerns the nine supernatural "manifestations of the Spirit." All nine of these gifts of the Spirit, according to the above-cited Scripture context, are FOR THE COMMON GOOD, that is to say, they are primarily manifested in the public forum, for the corporate benefit of those assembled. The implied import is that these manifestations are most likely to be manifested in the *public*, typically congregational, forum ("where two or three are gathered together in My name") as opposed to the *private* and *personal* life of an individual believer, though that by no means infers that manifestation in the latter scenario is precluded or prohibited.

It is in this public congregational forum that the manifestations of the Spirit are most frequently and commonly manifested and demonstrated. For instance, the working of miracles, the gifts of healings, and faith seem to be activated and manifested more commonly "where two or three are gathered together," for "the COMMON good," than they are in the personal life of an individual for the "private" benefit of that individual. This demonstrates the importance of the corporate anointing (Jn. 14:12).

The verses immediately following the listing of the Manifestations of the Spirit (1 Cor. 12:12-27) seem to be focusing on and emphasizing this matter of these manifestations being especially operational in the corporate Body of Christ, which, though it consists of individual members, is individual members related to and needful of one another and assembled together corporately. "But one and the same Spirit works all these things (the Manifestations of the Spirit), distributing to each one individually *as He wills.*" The "will" of the Spirit seems to encompass an especial preference for distributing these manifestations and causing them to operate as the corporate Body of Christ congregates together, reinforcing the Lord's insistence that we be continually cognizant of our need for one another (cf., 1 Cor. 12:21). For instance, while it is possible for a sick believer to lay hands upon himself and effect healing or recovery, that seems to be a less common occurrence; rather, it seems that healing virtue is more often released into the body of the infirmed through the laying on of hands by another believer.

The Function of the Charismata or Charismatic Gifts

The Charismatic Wind that began to blow across Christendom in 1960 came to activate believers who would believe and receive the Holy Spirit and His manifestation gifts in the operation of His supernatural POWER. The effect of the Baptism in the Holy Spirit, the promise of the Father (Ac. 1:4-5), which Jesus bestows upon every believer who will but ask Him (Mat. 3:11, Lk. 11:13), is that "when the Holy Spirit has come upon you, you will receive

POWER to TESTIFY about me with great effect" (Ac. 1:8, L.B.). It is "POWER" to be "witnesses" of Jesus to a lost and dying world that is bestowed upon believers when they receive the Baptism in the Holy Spirit.

The Greek word translated "power" in this text and others in the New Testament is "*dunamis*," which connotes "SUPERNATURAL ENABLEMENT." Thus, the import of Jesus' statement is that with the Baptism of the Holy Spirit we receive supernatural enablement to be vessels for the manifestations of the Spirit through us in order to give testimony of the viability of the resurrection power of Jesus! Upon being endowed with power from on high, Spirit-baptized believers become witnesses of Jesus primarily to the world.

The Ministry Gifts

"And there are varieties of MINISTRIES, but the same LORD." (1 Cor. 12:5)

The "Lord" and Head of the Church, Jesus Christ, endows "some" (Eph. 4:11) select believers of His choosing with HIS MINISTRY GIFTS for the *spiritual* development (edification and education) and governance (non-authoritarian steerage, pilotage) of the Church. When He was baptized in the Spirit, Jesus Himself was endowed with these giftings by the Father and operated them during His fleshly ministry. Thus, in that they were bestowed unto Him by the Father, through the Helper, the Holy Spirit, they are HIS, the Lord's giftings as the Head of the Church to bestow upon whomever He wills and chooses. It is vital to understand that it is the LORD, who is the *functional* Head of the Church, as opposed to human hierarchies, and as such **He** appoints whomever **HE** elects to these offices of function, and anoints them with these supernatural enablements. Only "some," not "all" (cf., 1 Cor. 12:28ff) believers are so appointed and anointed. This set of giftings, also known as the Fivefold Ministry Offices (functions), is delineated and their functions are explained in Ephesians 4:7-13. They are FIVE (the number in Scripture for divinely bestowed giftings of grace) in number, which are: apostles, prophets, evangelists, pastors, and teachers.

The Motivation Gifts

> And there are varieties of EFFECTS (OPERATIONS, KJV; ENERGIZINGS, lit. Gr.), but the same GOD who works all these things *in all persons*. (1 Cor. 12:6)

GOD THE FATHER bestows the MOTIVATION GIFTS, which "energize" (literal meaning of "function" [NASB] and "office" [KJV] in Romans 12:4) each individual believer with a specific function or ability, and is the believer's primary motivation in life, whether discovered or undiscovered by the person. These "energizings" are innate talents, abilities, or enablements God the Father infuses into the internal makeup of people, and, I believe, become especially viable when individuals become a "new creature" in Christ by virtue of the infusion of the Holy Spirit at the New Birth. While some believers may be able to function in some degree in a number of these giftings, there is always ONE which motivates (moves, energizes, impels) them primarily. These gifts are delineated in Romans 12:4-8. They are SEVEN (the number of the Father's Sovereignty and Perfection) in number, which are: prophecy, serving, teaching, exhorting, giving, ruling, showing of mercy.

It is vital that the Body of Christ, individually and collectively, understand the critical differences between these giftings, offices, and functions; especially the differences between the *Manifestation* Gifts and the *Ministry* Gifts. One of the things that much of the Body has been confused about is the difference between the transient "power" [dunamis, Gr.] (cf., Ac. 1:8) distributed by the Holy Spirit, according to His will, unto believers to "minister" unto others, and the "authority" [exousia, Gr.] inherent in the Fivefold Ministry Offices (functions) with which the Lord as Head of the Church anoints believers of His election and appointment. This widespread confusion and lack of knowledge regarding these two separate and distinct matters has produced untold problems and wreaked incalculable spiritual damage in the past. Great, in this hour of rampant deception from "deceiving spirits and doctrines of demons by the means of the hypocrisy of liars" (1 Tim. 4:1-2), is the Church's need for clear, unambiguous, precise, and authoritative (i.e., apostolic) teaching regarding these graces lavishly bestowed by the Triune-God unto the co-sovereign Betrothed of Christ, the Lamb's Wife! So desperate is Her need to appropriate and assimilate all the supernatural grace God is dispensing in these "perilous times" that are made so because men have become:

> lovers of self, lovers of money, boastful, arrogant, revilers, disobedient to parents, ungrateful, unholy, unloving, irreconcilable, malicious gossips, without self-control, brutal, haters of good, treacherous, reckless, conceited, lovers of pleasure rather than lovers of God, holding to a form of godliness, although they have denied its power; Avoid such men as these. For among them are those who enter into households and captivate weak women weighed down with sins, led on by various impulses, always learning and never able to come to the knowledge of the truth. (1 Tim. 3:1-7)

The Gradual De-emphasis of the Gifts of the Spirit

In retrospect, it can be observed that while most true Pentecostal groups and denominations that formed out of it professed an espousal of all nine of the Manifestation Gifts of the Spirit, the primary emphasis of the Pentecostal Movement (c., 1906) was the Prophetic or Vocal Gifts—tongues, interpretation of tongues, and prophecy. While there were some operations in the Revelation (word of wisdom, word of knowledge, and discerning of spirits) and Power (healing, miracles, and faith) gifts during the Pentecostal Movement, especially at its inception, in the passage of time, fewer and fewer Pentecostal congregations ascribed significant importance to these latter two sets of Charismata.

The overall effect of this gradual de-emphasis has been that at present, going on a decade past the Pentecostal Movement's centennial mark, there is little *mention*, let alone *manifestation*, of the Revelation and Power Gifts in the meetings of classic Pentecostal churches. In fact, the stark reality is that today, anyone attempting to operate in these gifts in the vast majority of Pentecostal denominations will be met with an Antarctic-like blast of frigid resistance and contempt. Sadly, over the more than one-hundred years of classic Pentecostalism that have transpired, those denominations and their churches who once were the enthusiastic champions of the Charismata, have transitioned from tenacious belief to tacit tolerance to outright disbelief and disdain for the Manifestations of the Spirit.

Unfortunately, the sad scenario as we stand in the second decade of the 21st Century is that if you raise your voice above a whisper in prayer, worship, or vocalization of your "prayer language" in most Pentecostal church services, as was so common during the first fifty years or so of the Pentecostal Movement, chances are you will be remonstrated by the ushers, and if you continue these "loud outbursts that are disturbing to some of our less demonstrative congregants who don't embrace this kind of worship" in future services you will eventually be told that you are unwelcome in the church. So fair warning: If you receive this glorious Baptism in the Holy Spirit that releases the "rivers of Living Water" of the Holy Spirit through you, you will have to be discriminating as to what church you attend.

A Time of Refreshing and Period of Restoration

Reviewing the history briefly to see how things progressed to where we are today, at the approximate apex of the American Pentecostal Movement, as enthusiasm for and espousal of the Manifestations of the Spirit, and consequently the influence of Pentecostalism, was waning, a powerful new Wind of the Spirit began to blow in the 1960s, which became known as the *Charismatic Movement*. This move of the Spirit not only brought forth a desperately needed "time of refreshing" (Ac. 3:19) from the presence of the Lord, but it was also a sovereignly produced, foreordained "period of restoration" (Ac. 3:21) by God, in which a "recovery" and a "rediscovery" of the nine "manifestations of the Spirit" (also referred to as "the charismata" or "charismatic gifts") listed in First Corinthians 12:7-11 was effected.

At its inception, the Charismatic Movement (c., 1960) was a divinely orchestrated Wind and Working of the Spirit, the primary purpose of which was to bring forth a restoration of and renewed awareness in the "Charismata" or Manifestation Gifts of the Spirit. Secondarily, it was also one of the God-initiated "times of refreshing" that "come from **the presence** of the Lord" (Ac. 3:19), which, at least during the 20th Century seemed to emerge approximately every twenty years. Through that Movement, God was announcing that the Manifestations of the Spirit were not relegated to and "passed away" with some by-gone era of long ago, but that "Jesus Christ is the same today, yesterday, and forever" (Heb.13:8), and that God changes not (Mal. 3:6)! What He *was* in any era, He *IS*, and what He *is*, He always has been and always will be—for He is the Great "I Am"—God the Eternal and Eternally God!

The rediscovery of the Manifestations of the Spirit demonstrated once again that it was not *God* who had changed over the centuries of Church history, but the *Church*, or perhaps more appropriately, the beliefs, doctrines, and operations of the Church. But, that should not be surprising considering that not since the end of the 2nd Century A.D. has the Church actively and earnestly labored to fulfill all five of the Lord's final commandments preceding His ascension into Heaven to take His Seat at the Right Hand of God—i.e., "The Great Commission" (Mk. 16:15-18).

Despair Not! God is Restoring!

But, despair not, you of the True Remnant Church Jesus is building! God is not finished yet with all of this! God Himself will yet bring forth His justice and judgment upon these corrupt ecclesiastical coalitions of hubristic human interlopers! He is about to identify and separate the wheat from the tares, the false shepherds and sheep, from the true. God will not be mocked! Blasphemy against the Holy

Spirit and His workings is still the one sin that is such an affront unto God that it shall never be forgiven! The Gifts of the Holy Spirit are still given by the One True Spirit of God, and God will not allow what is Good, which only He can author, to be seen and spoken of as evil!

Be not discouraged or dismayed! Continue to heed the commandment of the Spirit to "Pursue love, yet earnestly desire (covet, KJV) *spiritual gifts*, but ESPECIALLY THAT YOU MAY PROPHESY...(for) one who prophesies (i.e., exercises the Vocal Gifts: tongues, interpretation of tongues, prophecy) speaks to men for edification, exhortation, and consolation (encouragement)...one who prophesies EDIFIES (charges up as a battery is charged up) THE CHURCH" (1 Cor. 12:1-4). God knows, now more than ever before, the true remnant Church Jesus is building (Zech. 12:7-9; Mat. 16:18) needs all the edification, exhortation, and encouragement the Spirit desires to bestow upon a battle-weary and dismayed Church through the Manifestations of the Spirit, which are given for the "COMMON GOOD" of the Church (1 Cor. 12:7)!

Chapter Thirteen
Tongues & Interpretation of Tongues

"And <u>God</u> has **APPOINTED in the church**...*various* **kinds of tongues**" (1 Cor. 12:28, NASB).

"And <u>God</u> hath **SET...in the church...diversities of tongues**" (1 Cor. 12:28, KJV).

I want to now take a brief look at the one Manifestation Gift that has been at the center of the greatest amount of heated controversy of all the Charismatic Giftings—the matter of what the King James Version renders as "diversities of tongues."

To properly understand this whole matter of "various kinds of tongues," as the New American Standard Bible renders it, requires to first understand the matter of tongues is not a humanly-invented phenomenon, but as the above passage brings out, it was God's idea and doing to *appoint* or *set* in the *ekklesia* or Church Jesus is building different "kinds of tongues." The terms "set" and "appointed" both connote permanence. Everyone who has ever worked with cement knows well what the word "set" means, and that once the mixture is set it is permanent and immutable. So, this use by the Holy Spirit of these terms in this passage establishes that fact that God has ordained that various kinds of tongues should be operating in the assemblies of the Church for as long as the Church exists. Nowhere does Scripture inform us that God has rescinded the appointment of the gift of various forms of tongues in the Church, though many have sought to have them "impeached" or "abrogated" from the Church without any Biblical justification for doing so. Cessationists must resort to extra-biblical theorization to support their unproven assertions, which are based virtually exclusively and entirely upon past Church history, which is the record of what the Church *did* vis-à-vis what God ordained and prescribed in His Word for the Church to do. The chasm between the two is vast!

The second crucial matter that must be established in examining this issue is that there are two distinct and separate manifestations or functions of tongues. Most of the confusion and distortion regarding tongues is rooted in the mixing of these two separate forms of tongues together in terms of function and Biblical "rules" for their function. It is the tangled blob that results from such incorrect confluence I hope to untangle in this chapter.

The first form of tongues is tongues in the *personal* prayer and praise expressions of a believer who has been baptized in the Holy Spirit, such as it occurred on the Day of Pentecost, in which case the devout Jewish observers present that day heard the 120 Spirit-immersed disciples "in our *own* tongues speaking of the mighty deeds of God," which event "bewildered" and wrought such "amazement and great perplexity" in them that they began saying among themselves, "What does this mean?" (Ac. 2:1-12). That bewilderment and great perplexity continues yet today for myriads who have not themselves received of the outpouring of the Spirit.

The other manifestation of tongues is a *public* form that occurs in a public forum. We'll look at that form after looking at the private and personal expression of tongues in prayer and praise.

Tongues in the Form of Prayer and Praise

"For if I PRAY in a tongue, my spirit PRAYS, but my mind is unfruitful. What is the outcome then? I shall PRAY with the spirit and I shall PRAY with the mind also; I shall sing (Praise) with the spirit and I shall sing with the mind also." (1 Cor. 14:14-15)

Though appearing in the context concerning the proper operation of the Manifestations of the Spirit in the congregational forum, the above verses DO NOT pertain to the Manifestation Gift of "SPEAKING" in tongues, but rather to the **personal prayer and praise language in tongues**. These verses and the preceding verse (v. 13) are the only times the Greek word *proseuchomai* (pray) is used in the 14th Chapter of First Corinthians. The matter of "praying in the Spirit" is mentioned here in connection with verse 13 (note the prefatory word "for" at the beginning of the verse) to illustrate the fact that when a person speaks in an "unknown tongue" an interpretation is needful because his "mind (intellect) is unfruitful"—in other words, his mind does not understand what has been said in the tongue that is unknown to him. All the rest of the usages of the word "tongues" is in connection with the Greek word "laleo" (speak). The word "speak" carries with it the connotation "to speak a message."

Instructions pertaining to the orderly operation of "tongues" given in the dissertation of First Corinthians 12 and 14 are NOT references to the **personal prayer and praise language** received by believers baptized in the Spirit (Ac. 2:1-11; 10:44-46; 19:16; Rom. 12:26-27; et al.); rather, they pertain to the congregational or public Manifestation of the Spirit of "tongues" along with its required accompanying interpretation of tongues. Ground rules for the orderly operation of the Manifestation Gifts are necessary only for their operation in the congregational forum, since it would be difficult for one to be "out of order" in the operation of the Manifestations of the Spirit in his/her private prayer and praise exercise. Indeed, it would be hard to imagine a scenario in which praying, praising, or singing "in the Spirit" (in tongues) privately could possibly ever be "out of order."

> "If anyone SPEAKS (*laleo*, Gr.) in a tongue...let one INTERPRET...." (1 Cor. 14:27)

Every Spirit-inspired message spoken on behalf of God in the congregational forum (i.e., *prophecy*, not prayer or praise) must be accompanied with interpretation into the common language of the hearers, because it is a message from God to the assembly, which cannot be understood unless it is interpreted into the common language of the hearers (1 Cor. 14:6-17). If tongues are not interpreted by someone operating in the Manifestation Gift of interpretation of tongues then it is not *prophecy* (a message from God to the congregation), but *prayer and praise*. Only tongues interpreted into the common language of the hearers enabling them to understand the message and be edified by it is prophecy.

> "Therefore let one who SPEAKS in a tongue pray that he may interpret...but if there is no interpreter, *let him keep silent* IN THE CHURCH; and let him *speak* to himself and to God." (1 Cor. 14:13,28)

Messages in tongues should only be given in a public forum, i.e., in an assembly, when "one who interprets" is present, which may be the speaker himself/herself. Notice that this passage is specifically talking about "one who SPEAKS in a tongue...IN THE CHURCH." It is not talking about when a person is offering up expressions of worship and praise and prayer out loud so that it can be heard by others. Such exultations do not have to be interpreted, because the person is speaking to God, not to people.

If no interpreter is present, then the person who has received a message from God should either pray for the interpretation if he/she is accustomed to interpreting messages in tongues, or he should keep silent in the church assembly and "speak (that message) to himself" and use his tongue to praise God, rather than to give the message to the entire congregation.

> "For one who speaks in a TONGUE does not speak to men, but to God...." (1 Cor. 14:2)

Taken out of its full context (verses 1-5), it could appear this verse is saying that a person who speaks in tongues is speaking to God and not to men, that is, he is not speaking a message from God to the assembly. However, when coupled with the entire context, as well as when it is connected with the information contained in the rest of the chapter, it becomes clear that what is being said is that an utterance in tongues without the required interpretation in the congregational forum is directed to God as prayer and praise.

"...*for no one understands*, but IN HIS SPIRIT he speaks mysteries...." (1 Cor. 14:2)

The rest of this verse makes it clear that the reason a person speaking in a tongue without interpretation is speaking to God is because "no one understands," and utterances in tongues spoken in the assembly as the first half of a prophetic message is intended to be understood by the entire congregation, which is why interpretation of tongues is then necessary and required.

Notice also the phrase "in his SPIRIT." This is where a message from God communicated in tongues is initially received—within the human spirit of the recipient. It is God communicating through the Holy Spirit to the human spirit of the person receiving the message. It is incumbent upon that person to then determine if this is a message that God wants communicated to the entire congregation. If there is not an interpreter present to interpret the message in tongues to the congregation (see below), then the person receiving the message in tongues "in his spirit" should "keep silent IN THE CHURCH (assembly)" and should "speak to himself and to God" (1 Cor. 14:28). If the message would be harmonious with the flow of the Spirit in that service, and would be "in order" in every other way, then the person should give the message in tongues, in order for it to be interpreted to the congregation. When the message in tongues is interpreted, it is no longer "a mystery"—that is the purpose of interpretation of tongues.

So, one is speaking to GOD in a tongue—that is, praying or praising—when there is no interpretation of the message into the common tongue of the congregation so that they all may understand and thus be edified. A message spoken in tongues in the congregational usage is one half of prophecy, for tongues *with* interpretation IS prophecy. I have found in teaching on this matter that people sometimes grasp and remember the concept better when it's put into formulaic language:

Formula: Tongues + Interpretation = Prophecy

All of this becomes even clearer when the first part of the full context is connected with the last part of the full context, in which case the following is the result:

> "For one who speaks in a *tongue* (without interpretation) does not speak to men, but to God; for no one understands, but in his spirit he speaks mysteries...UNLESS HE INTERPRETS, so that THE CHURCH may receive EDIFYING." (1 Cor. 14:25)

A person speaking in a tongue is speaking to God in prayer and praise unless his message is interpreted, in which case what he spoke is then a message from God to men, or the people present in the assembly, for the purposes of the spiritual edification of the congregation present, in which case the message becomes prophecy:

> "For one who speaks in a tongue does not speak to men, but to God; for no one understands, but in his spirit he speaks mysteries. *But one who prophesies SPEAKS TO MEN...one who prophesies edifies THE CHURCH....*" (1 Cor. 14:24)

Tongues in the Form of Message from God to an Assembly

The Manifestation Gift of Tongues in the form of a message to an assembly can be defined as a supernatural God-inspired, ecstatic message spoken through a believer in a language unknown to the speaker and not commonly known to the hearers for the spiritual edification of the assembly that must be interpreted into the common language of the hearers present in the assembly.

> "For one who speaks in a tongue does not speak to men, but to God; for no one understands, but in his spirit he speaks mysteries. But one who prophesies speaks to men... one who prophesies edifies the church...*and greater is one who PROPHESIES than one who SPEAKS IN TONGUES, UNLESS HE INTERPRETS*...." (1 Cor. 14:2-5)

It is in verse 5 of the above Scripture that we find the explanation, as mentioned before, that *tongues with interpre-*

tation is EQUIVALENT to and a form of <u>PROPHECY</u>. Again, the concept could be stated in formulaic terms as:

Tongues + Interpretation = Prophecy.

Conversely, because a message in tongues **must** be interpreted in order to be a proper prophetic utterance in the congregational usage, the following would also be an accurate description in formulaic language of utterances in tongues that are not interpreted:

Tongues – (minus) Interpretation = Prayer and Praise.

Tongues Should Not Be Hindered or Forbidden

"...do not **forbid** to speak in tongues." (1 Cor. 14:39)

To forbid believers to speak in tongues, as many denominations and churches do, is to forbid *God from speaking*, for tongues is a message *from God* inspired by the Holy Spirit and manifested through a human spokesperson.

No one has authority from the Scripture to forbid the speaking forth of tongues as a God-inspired message from God in a service that is done "decently and in order" (1 Cor. 14:40). Those who try to in any way hinder, suppress, restrict, demean, belittle, prevent, prohibit, or stop the free operation of this manifestation of the Spirit, does so against God Himself and the Holy Spirit, since it was God's appointment or ordination in the Church, and since tongues is a manifestation of the Holy Spirit Himself and not of any human. Those who engage in these acts against the Holy Spirit often approach committing and sometimes do commit sin against the Holy Spirit, which Jesus said would never be forgiven (Mk. 3:28-29).

The Function and Fruit of Tongues

"So then tongues are for a SIGN...to UNBELIEVERS." (1 Cor. 14:22)

The manifestation of tongues in an assembly is a supernatural "sign" especially to UNBELIEVERS (which, however, in no way infers that it is not to be manifested where only unbelievers are present) that has the same function and bears the same fruit as the gift of prophecy.

Primary Focus of the Fourteenth Chapter of First Corinthians

Since in all practicality it is virtually impossible for an individual believer to operate these manifestations of the Spirit in any manner other than "decently and in order" in personal and private prayer and praise, the primary focus of the instruction given in First Corinthians 14 must be concerning their operation in the congregational forum. The purpose and objective of this entire chapter is, indeed, inherent in the final and summational verse of the chapter, essentially proving they are a delineation of the rules effecting the proper and orderly operation of these "manifestations of the Spirit."

The Manifestation Gift of Interpretation of Tongues

Simply defined, the Manifestation Gift of Interpretation of Tongues (manifested in the congregational forum) is a supernatural God-inspired interpretation into the common language of the hearers of a message given in tongues. It is important to understand that an interpretation of tongues is not necessarily a verbatim (word-for-word) translation of the message given in tongues, but rather a verbal expression of the gist or overall essence of the message.

"If anyone SPEAKS in a tongue...let one INTERPRET" (1 Cor. 14:27)

Tongues given as one-half of a prophecy or prophetic word in an assembly must *always* be interpreted, but only once. This passage could well be setting the parameter also that there should be only one person doing the interpreting in a given service, as opposed to multiple interpreters, the purpose of which would be to limit the scope and maintain continuity of the thrust of messages given in a service.

Tongues expressed in the form of prayer and praise by individuals or any number of attendees of a given service do not require interpretation because what is being expressed is being expressed to God and not to the congregants. This fact nullifies the theory given by some that praising and praying to God out loud in a service, such as commonly occurs in authentic Pentecostal and Charismatic services, is not of God because no interpretation is given.

> "For one who speaks in a tongue does not speak to men, but to God; for no one understands, but in his spirit he speaks mysteries. But one who prophesies speaks to men...one who prophesies edifies the church...*and greater is one who PROPHESIES than one who SPEAKS IN TONGUES, <u>UNLESS</u> HE INTERPRETS....*" (1 Cor. 14:25).

A message in tongues spoken aloud in an assembly that is then accompanied by an interpretation of tongues is equivalent to prophecy, and in fact, IS prophecy. While tongues are not to be in any way prohibited or even discouraged, or its significance and importance undermined, this passage indicates that prophesying, i.e., operating the Manifestation Gift of prophecy, is operating in a higher spiritual strata than simply speaking in a tongue, UNLESS the speaker also interprets the message uttered in tongues. When that happens, then we are back to the place indicated before in formulaic language: Tongues + Interpretation of Tongues = Prophecy.

An Under-valued, Underdeveloped, and Under-understood Gift

I, for one, am absolutely convinced that individual believers and the collective church have only barely scratched the surface of what the Lord wants to reveal to us regarding *all* of the Charismata, and their operations, as well as these two particular forms of the Vocal Gifts, namely, tongues and the Interpretation of Tongues. In a way, we may only be at the Kindergarten level, metaphorically speaking, when it comes to understanding the purposes and usages of these "Heavenly languages," what Paul *may* have been referring to in the "Love Chapter" when he spoke about "tongues of men and of *angels*" (1 Cor. 13:1). I personally believe that there are times when the tongues that are being spoken in by Spirit-baptized believers is indeed "tongues of angels," though it is at other times manifestly obvious that the tongues being spoken in are tongues of men, i.e., earthly, human languages. I've heard and discerned both. On rare occasions I knew by the Spirit without any doubt that I was hearing angelic tongues being spoken.

In my own prayer and praise times, I have spoken in various kinds of tongues; it's not always the same tongue. I've heard other Spirit-baptized believers speak in "divers kinds of tongues" as well, going from one language to another as they continued to speak in tongues unknown to them, yielding their tongue to the Lord, and the Spirit giving the utterance. There is one tongue I speak in most commonly, particularly when I first start speaking in tongues, but often as I continue to press in deeper and deeper to the Spirit, my tongue begins to speak in other languages, making utterances, not gibberish, but utterances that are obviously intelligible speech in some language and possibly some particular dialect of a language, spoken by *some* race or people *somewhere* on earth.

Moreover, when I pray in tongues, I've noticed that sometimes, not always, but often, I seem to begin to receive what I can only describe as revelation that seems to "float up," if you will, out of my spirit and into my mind so that I can "know" it or "understand" something I've never thought about or understood before. Certainly, in that respect, I can personally attest to what many Pentecostal/Charismatic forefathers have taught about tongues being the "open door" into the Spirit realm.

I almost always begin to speak in tongues when I am about to minister in the Spirit, especially when I am wanting to "search the mind of the Spirit" for a prophetic word for someone, or when the Lord begins to prompt me that He has a prophetic word He wants to speak to someone through me. In either case, as I begin to pray and praise in tongues, or sometimes that prayer and praise begins to turn into what I am aware is a message in tongues, as I continue, I begin to receive an obvious and specific unction of the Spirit—an "unction for function"—to speak or do something that I am very aware is not me or originating from me or my mind, something supernatural—a manifestation of the Spirit—begins to happen through me. It could be a prophetic word, it could be to step out in the supernatural gift of faith to minister healing or deliverance to someone present who needs a miracle.

Tongues are a supernatural catalyst and open door into the Spirit realm, there is no doubt. It also is a "dynamo of the Spirit" in just the way that Jude expressed it, that you build or charge yourself up on your most holy faith by praying in the Spirit, meaning in tongues (Jude 20). Myriads of others who've experienced this can testify as well that this is how it works. It's supernatural! It cannot be explained or understood with the carnal mind or intellect, indeed, it by-passes the human intellect—it just works!

Nevertheless, as much as we DO "know" or understand about these matters, yet, there are galaxies of truth and understanding we do NOT possess about the supernatural gifts of the Spirit of tongues and interpretation of tongues. I am praying that God will begin to release some of that revelation that has been heretofore held in abeyance, more than likely because He has not yet been able to entrust that revelation unto the Church Jesus is building due to our overall lack of spiritual maturity, carnality, and continued self-centeredness. I'm praying this will all soon begin to change. I'm eager and anxious to see what God can do with and through a Church of genuine sold-out, died-to-self, flesh-crucified, obedient, Bible-believing, faith-walking, Spirit-infused, and Spirit-immersed believers! I'll be overjoyed when we can begin to throw off, divest, ourselves of the outer garments of religious garb and clothe ourselves with the garments of the Spirit, wrapping our necks with the mantle of the Vocal gifts, anointing the entire Body of Christ as Spokespersons of the Spirit to speak Spirit-inspired messages of salvation and deliverance to a lost and dying world and Spirit-inspired messages of liberation and exaltation to an all-too passive and largely impassive Church.

A Profoundly Powerful Illustration

Several years ago I was attending a particularly Spirit-anointed Sunday Morning church service in which the

Tongues & Interpretation of Tongues 149

guest speaker was a Pentecostal pastor who related one of the most awesome and awe-inspiring stories I ever recall hearing involving the matter of tongues and interpretation of tongues, and the combination of the two producing a prophetic message to the believer/speaker. One Sunday night after preaching as a guest preacher in a town about 300 miles away from his home, he had decided to drive home rather than stay overnight in a hotel room and drive home the next day. For some reason he didn't understand, he just had a strong internal desire to do that, even though it meant getting home around 3:00 A.M.

When he was only a few minutes away from his exit to home off the interstate, a few minutes before 2:00 A.M., there was one of those signs you see all along the interstate informing about an exit to a highway that intersected with the interstate about 10 miles ahead, with those little images indicating the types of services available at that exit—gas stations, stores, restaurants, et cetera. For the last hour, he had been having an unusually anointed time of praying and praising God in tongues. As he was just approaching the sign, a "thought" kind of floated up from his spirit that said, "Turn off at that exit and get gas." Well, he thought that was kind of weird because he had been monitoring his gas gauge regularly all along the trip he had traveled many times before, and he knew he had plenty of gas—just a little less than a quarter of a tank—to make it home less than 30 miles ahead. So, he basically dismissed the "thought" and chalked it up to being exhausted and it being nearly 2-O'clock in the morning, and continued praying and praising in tongues.

But, when he got to the sign at the 5-mile mark from the same exit, that "thought" popped up again: "Turn off at that exit and get gas." Again he looked at his gas gauge, and said to himself (he thought), "I don't need gas; I've got plenty to make it home." Again, he blew off the "nonsensical" thought, and went back to praying and praising in tongues.

At the 1-mile mark, the same thing happened again! When he got to the exit, he could literally feel his arms fighting to keep going straight and not turn off at that exit, because his mind was telling him it made absolutely no sense! But, at the last second, it was as if someone else took hold of the steering wheel and he could do nothing but watch as his vehicle slowly swerved to take that exit.

When he got to the intersection, there was only one sign for a convenience store with gas pumps, so he turned in that direction, came to the store, pulled in, and knowing he did not need gas, went around the gas pumps and pulled into a parking space at the front of the store. He said to himself, "What am I doing here?" He didn't know the answer. But, he thought, "Well, I do have to go to the bathroom," so he got out went in, spotted the bathroom signs, and went to the bathroom. When he came in, he made a quick glance to the counter, and saw a lone woman attendant there, who was obviously counting the cash in the drawer, apparently to close the store at 2:00 A.M. He said a terse, "Hello," as he went toward the bathrooms, to which the woman replied likewise. All the while in the bathroom he kept saying to himself, "Why am I here? Why am I here? I don't know why I'm here."

When he came out of the bathroom, though his mind was telling him to get back in the car and start driving home again, something wouldn't let him leave. With his hands in his pockets, tie loosened, sleeves of his white "preacher" shirt rolled up, he just started slowly meandering around the store looking to see if some little snack-item seemed appealing to buy to justifying his coming in and using the bathroom. The female clerk just continued to do what she was doing, not paying much attention to him.

Finally, she said, "Sir, can I help you with something?" Without missing a beat, he said he heard himself responding, "Yes, can you tell me why I'm here?" He was a little shocked he had said that, and the woman responded, "What do you mean?" Then he found himself responding,

"Well, I'm a Pentecostal preacher on my way home in the middle of the night after preaching all day, and I was praying in tongues—that's what we Pentecostals do—and three times a word came to me to take this exit and get gas, even though I don't need gas and have plenty to make it home; can you tell me why I'm here?"

The woman immediately burst into tears, dropped the money in her hands, and said, "Yes, sir, I can tell you why you're here!" And, with that she reached down under the counter and pulled out a .357 Magnum handgun, and through her sobs confessed, "Today, I became so despondent and depressed, and saw no way out of my problems, dropped my daughter off at my mother's, and I had decided that after I closed the store tonight here at 2:00 A.M. and made the bank deposit at the bank down the street, I was going to take this gun I just bought yesterday and kill myself!"

The preacher said, "Yes, honey, that's why I'm here; you don't need to do that; God sent me here to save your life, and to lead you into the arms of the Savior, His son, Jesus." And he prayed with her, and led her to the Lord, took the gun, followed her to her mother's house, and continued on his journey home, with a heart overflowing with awe, wonder, amazement, and thankfulness for the supernatural gift of tongues and interpretation of tongues, thinking to himself what the Apostle Paul wrote to the Corinthians, "I thank God that I speak in tongues more than you all!"

Tongues with interpretation of tongues is prophecy, and God so desperately desires to speak to us messages straight from His heart of Love!

"The thief (Satan) came but for to steal, kill, and destroy! I came that you might have life, and have it more abundantly!" said Jesus, the Savior of all Mankind (Jn. 10:10).

CHAPTER FOURTEEN
CESSATIONISM REFUTED

My good friend, Charles Carrin, as a Baptist pastor for more than twenty-eight years, was much like Apollos before Priscilla and Aquila "took him aside and explained to him the way of God more accurately" (Ac. 18:24-26). Like Apollos, he was "an eloquent man...and he was mighty in the Scriptures," he "had been instructed in the way of the Lord" in Presbyterian seminary, was "fervent in spirit," and "was speaking and teaching accurately the things concerning Jesus," meaning the Gospel of Christ's sacrifice. However, Charles, like Apollos and myriad other sincere and fervent traditional denominational ministers today, was "acquainted only with the baptism of John," the original Baptist.

This simply was the way it was for this well-spoken and well-studied hyper-Calvinist Bible expositor and Primitive Baptist pastor for nearly three decades of service spanning the final half of the twentieth century, who, true to his denomination's beliefs, denied the miraculous works of the Holy Spirit, until one day in his twenty-ninth year of ministry when, in the midst of an extended period of spiritual dryness and emptiness brought on by a severe personal trial, he had a personal encounter with the Holy Spirit, and despite all his refutations, protestations, and contrarian beliefs, was thoroughly immersed or baptized in both the water and the fire of the Holy Spirit! Instantaneously, he and his theology were forever changed! Straightaway, cessation theories for Charles Carrin were thoroughly expunged from his belief system, but more importantly, from his personal relationship with the Godhead. From that day forward, he had no more questions regarding the reality of

Cessationism Refuted 153

the Baptism in the Holy Spirit; no not one!

The horrendous tragedy Charles suffered through forced him to acknowledge a plethora of Scriptures he had previously been blinded to or ignored. It was a time of intense personal pain and testing. The truths he saw once, like Saul of Tarsus when Ananias laid his hands upon him, the spiritual scales fell from his eyes, were frightening; they had power to destroy his denominational ministry, and at that point he had no way of knowing that another, more wondrous and extensive ministry awaited him. As a result of his submitting to God in that crisis, Charles emerged with an amazing anointing of the Holy Spirit. Today, his ministry centers upon the visible demonstration of the Spirit and imparting of His gifts.

After eighty-three years of living and over sixty-five in the Kingdom (at the time of this writing), Charles has come to some specific conclusions concerning what the Spirit says in the Word of God about the Baptism in the Holy Spirit, as well as the Dunamis-Power of God unto supernatural manifestations of the Spirit throughout the Church Age. This learned and articulate servant of God, in the following excerpt of one of his recent articles, does a masterful job of refuting the wholly indefensible cessation theories espoused by many so-called "fundamentalist" denominations today, who, unfortunately, continue to "invalidate the Word of God by their traditions." I was so impressed with the capturing of the essence of the matter by this inveterate minister, I basically prevailed upon him to gain his permission to include it in this book, which he, fortunately for readers and listeners, graciously granted me.

Kingdom Faith or Kingdom Fiction? (By Charles Carrin)

The New Testament gospel is powerful, eternal, and perpetually true. Two-thousand years after its presentation to the world it is still relevant, unabridged, and unchallengeable. When Charles Spurgeon was asked how he defended the gospel, he replied, "I don't defend the gospel any more than I would defend a lion. I just open the cage and let it out."

Jesus called His message the "gospel of the Kingdom." That message has never been, nor will ever be changed. Nor will it become a gospel of the church. The Kingdom knows no failure. The Kingdom is triumphant, victorious, all-conquering. The Kingdom is permanent, unchanging. The Kingdom needs no such excuse to absolve herself of blame.

The church is subject to great failure. The church is schismatic, self-indulging, and unreliable. The church is temporal, justifies herself and vindicates her failures. The church has invented an escape-hatch called *Cessation Theology*. This pleasant sounding expression declares that God has withdrawn the Holy Spirit's miraculous power from the church. The church has a book—the Bible—and little more than that. We have no power because God has removed it (so the modern Church says). The fault is not ours.

Much of modern, evangelical Christianity is a parallel of the ministry of Apollos. It is sincere, eloquent, accurately teaching Bible truth as far as it allows itself to believe. But its doctrine is measured by its own opinion–it is afraid to measure its doctrine by Scripture.

Dispensationalism—the claim that miraculous gifts of the Holy Spirit passed away—dominates traditional Christianity. Jesus said there would be no such change. Hear His words:

> "All authority has been given to Me in heaven and on earth. Go therefore and make disciples of all the nations, baptizing them in the name of the Father and of the Son and of the Holy Spirit, teaching them to observe all things that I have commanded you; and lo, I am with you always, even to the end of the age."(Mat. 28:18-20)

Jesus fully expected the church "at the end of the age" to believe and teach "all things" that He had commanded the original disciples.

The Apostle Jude did not believe the cessationism claim. Instead, he presented one of the New Testament's

Cessationism Refuted

strongest defenses for the Gospel's inalterability. He said, "I found it necessary to write to you exhorting you to contend earnestly for the faith which was once for all delivered to the saints" (Jude 3). The "once for all" in our English Bibles comes from a valuable little Greek word, *"hapax."* In spite of its small size, *hapax* carries significant authority. It means: "one, a single time, conclusively, absolutely all, every one."

This *hapax*-expression appears at least eight times in the Greek New Testament. It is translated "once for all" five times in the New King James Version. Three additional times the New International Version translates it as "once." In every instance *hapax* establishes the unchangeability of its subject. Six of the references below apply directly to Jesus, one applies to the believer, and the final one to Kingdom faith. In four instances in the Greek text the preposition "epi" (upon) is added to reinforce the "once for all" meaning.

The Hapax Scriptures

1. Romans 6:10 "For the death that Jesus died, He died to sin *once for all*; but the life that He lives, He lives to God."

2. Hebrews 7:27 "Who does not need daily, as those high priests, to offer up sacrifices, first for His own sins and then for the people's, for this Jesus did *once for all* when He offered up Himself."

3. Hebrews 9:12 "Not with the blood of goats and calves, but with His own blood Jesus entered the Most Holy Place *once for all*, having obtained eternal redemption."

4. Hebrews 9:26-27 "He then would have had to suffer often since the foundation of the world; but now, *once* at the end of the ages, He has appeared to put away sin by the sacrifice of Himself."

5. Hebrews 10:2-3 For the worshipers, *once* purified, would have had no more consciousness of sins.

6. Hebrews 10:10 "By that will we have been sanctified through the offering of the body of Jesus Christ *once for all*."

7. 1 Peter 3:18 "For Christ also hath *once* suffered for sins, the just for the unjust, that he might bring us to God, being put to death in the flesh, but quickened by the Spirit."

8. Jude 3 "Beloved ... I found it necessary to write to you exhorting you to contend earnestly for the faith which was *once for all* delivered to the saints."

To which of these *hapax* –"once for all"—passages are you willing to apply Cessation Theology? Would your theology be complete if *any* of the "once for all" references were removed from the work of Jesus? Would you like *any* of these subjects to be vulnerable to change? Are you genuinely glad that they are *"hapax"* — "once for all"—secure? If so, it is *impossible* for you to endorse Cessation Theology. You cannot accept the works of Jesus as *hapax* and then deny the Holy Spirit the same respect in His maintaining *hapax* in the permanency of Scripture. You cannot do it and uphold integrity with the Word!

Modern Christianity has convinced itself that Jesus provided two distinct gospels and two distinct faiths—one for the First Century Church and one for those who followed after. The first was miraculously empowered; the second was not. The first had the baptismal gift of the Holy Spirit; the second was merely given a book telling what the Holy Spirit had achieved in the past. Hear the truth: Jesus provided everyone—past, present, future—with a faith which was *hapax*-true, *hapax*-strong, *hapax*-forever.

The fact is this: Whether you and I accept it or not, the original "faith that was once for all delivered to the saints" is still intact. It is unaltered. In a conclusive, unchangeable way the faith of the Apostolic Era was delivered for "all time" intact to every subsequent generation. There will *never* be another.

Someone argues, "But I have never seen the miraculous works of the Holy Spirit in my church!" True. But the fault lies with the *church*, not with *God*. The contemporary church is a victim of its own unbelief. It has created its blighted condition.

Cessationism Refuted 157

Observe that the Apostle Jude said he:
1. Found it "necessary";
2. To "exhort you";
3. To "contend earnestly."

This agrees perfectly with Jesus' instruction in Matthew 28:18-20 that believers to "the end of the age" be taught to "observe all things that I have commanded you" (the original disciples). Then, as if to emphasize the unchangeability of the gospel's time-span, He said, "Lo, I am with you always, even to the end of the age." Observe the expression "all things." What did He mean by that expression? Scripture does not leave us to wonder. Matthew 10:7-9 makes it very plain: "As you go, preach, saying, 'The kingdom of heaven is at hand.' Heal the sick, cleanse the lepers, raise the dead, cast out demons. Freely you have received, freely give." When He said, "teach them all things...to the end of the age," this is what He meant.

The obvious message is that the gospel—and the faith arising from it—have been permanently given *one time* and will never be given again. That initial provision is sufficient "once for all" time and "once for all" people. In an emphatic way, this says that New Testament faith, doctrinally and experientially, as it was originally presented by the Holy Spirit, is unchangeable. It cannot be added to or taken from. Any cessationist claim otherwise is a hoax. Such an accusation insults the Cross and the work of the Holy Spirit (cf., 2 Pet. 1:21).

Even so, the idea is rampant in modern Christianity that parts of the Covenant-Book which Jesus ratified by the sprinkling of His blood (Heb. 9:11-15), have lost validity. This supposedly occurred at the death of the Apostle John in 70 A.D., or when the New Testament books were canonized into one volume in 367 A.D.

The truth is: modern Christians have invented that monstrous idea. We have done so because we do not want accountability for our own failures. If we can justify the absence of God's miraculous presence by claiming He withdrew it from us, we don't have to accept blame for our having withdrawn ourselves from Him.

Jesus Said "The Scripture Cannot Be Broken"

> "Jesus answered them, 'Is it not written in your law*, 'I said, "You are gods'? If He called them gods, to whom the word of God came (and the Scripture cannot be broken), do you say of Him whom the Father sanctified and sent into the world, 'You are blaspheming,' because I said, 'I am the Son of God'? If I do not do the works of My Father, do not believe Me; but if I do, though you do not believe Me, believe the works, that you may know and believe that the Father is in Me, and I in Him. Therefore they sought again to seize Him, but He escaped out of their hand." (John 10:34-40) [*Psalm 82:6]

Jesus reminded the Jews that it was David—not Himself—who first wrote about God miraculously empowering the saints. Those fortunate ones to whom "the word of God comes" are so changed and endowed that in the eyes of the demonic-world—in a comparative sense—they become gods (with a little "g"). Simply stated, Jesus intended the saints to exercise power over the demonic realm (cf., Luke 10:19).

It was Jesus who said "The Scripture **CANNOT** be broken." That means that the New Testament is still intact. No part is outdated and it cannot be victimized by cessation teaching. In believing it we open ourselves to receive a miraculous imparting of its "word." Those to whom the Word of God comes are changed from *ordinary* humanity into *extraordinary* humanity. The "word of the Lord came" to Abraham, Samuel, Nathan, Gad, Solomon, Elijah, Elisha, Isaiah, Jeremiah, Ezekiel, Haggai, Zechariah, John the Baptist, the first disciples, others. All of these experienced transformation when the "word of God" came to them. This is the only sensible explanation for the explosive growth of Christianity in the Roman world.

What Happens Today When The True "Word of God" Comes With Power?

1. Psalm 107:19-20 "Then they cried unto the LORD in their trouble, and he saved them out of their distresses. He sent his word, and healed them, and delivered them from their destructions."

2. Matthew 8:16-17 "When evening had come, they brought unto him many who were demon-possessed. And He cast out the spirits with His word, and healed all who were sick: That it might be fulfilled which was spoken by Isaiah the prophet, saying, He Himself took our infirmities, and bore our sicknesses."

3. Luke 4:31-36 "Then He went down to Capernaum, a city of Galilee, and taught them on the Sabbath days. And they were astonished at his doctrine: for his word was with power. And in the synagogue there was a man, who had a spirit of an unclean demon, and he cried out with a loud voice, Saying, Let us alone; what have we to do with you, Jesus of Nazareth? Did you come to destroy us? I know you who you are—the Holy One of God. But Jesus rebuked him, saying, Be quiet and come out of him. And when the demon had thrown him in their midst, it came out of him, and did not hurt him. Then they were all amazed, and spoke among themselves, saying, What a word is this! For with authority and power he commands the unclean spirits, and they come out."

4. Acts 2:40-41 "And with many other words he testified and exhorted them, saying, Be saved from this perverse generation. Then those who gladly received his word were baptized; and that about three thousand souls were added unto them."

5. Titus 1:1-3 "Paul, a servant of God, and an apostle of Jesus Christ, according to the faith of God's elect, and the acknowledgment of the truth which accords with godliness; In hope of eternal life, which God, who cannot lie, promised before time began; But has in due times manifested his word through preaching, which was committed

to me according to the commandment of God our Savior."

6. 1 John 2:4-6. "He who says, I know him, and does not keep His commandments, is a liar, and the truth is not in him. But whoever keeps His word, truly the love of God is perfected in him: By this know we that we are in him. He who says he abides in Him ought himself also so to walk, even as he walked." (The "Word" is already perfected, so what is being perfected? The one who receives the word.)

7. Luke 1:38. Mary was impregnated when she told the angel, "Be it unto me according to your word."

8. Matthew 4:4. Jesus said: "But he answered and said, It is written, Man shall not live by bread alone, but by every word that proceedeth out of the mouth of God."

9. Matthew 24:35. Jesus said: "Heaven and earth shall pass a way but My words will by no means pass away."

10. God the Father said: "My Covenant I will not break nor alter the Word that is gone out of my lips." Psalm 89:34.

11. John 17:8. Jesus said to the Father: "For I have given to them (the disciples) the words which You have given Me, and they have received them...."

12. 1 Peter 1:25. Peter said: "But the word of the Lord endures forever. Now this is the word which by the gospel was preached to you."

13. 2 Peter 1:21. Peter said again: "Knowing this first, that no prophecy of Scripture is of any private interpretation, for prophecy never came by the will of man, but holy men of God spoke as they were moved by the Holy Spirit."

14. 2 Timothy 3:16. Paul said: "Be diligent...rightly diving the word of truth." II Timothy 2:1. Paul said again: "All Scripture is given by inspiration of God and is profitable."

15. Galatians 1:8. Paul said once more: "But even if we, or an angel from heaven, preach any other gospel to you than what we have preached to you, let him be accursed."

16. Psalm 119:89. David said: "Forever, O Lord, Your Word is settled in Heaven."

If you are one of those believers whose Cessation Theology denies the integrity of Scripture or the Holy Spirit's miraculous gifts, stop it! You are on the losing team! You are on God's opposing team!

Kingdom faith is *fact*, not *fiction*! *Hapax*—"once for all."

Chapter Fifteen
A Different Gospel — Void of Power

Each year, on a Sunday in May or June — fifty days after Resurrection Sunday (what many Christian denominations and sects insist on calling, "Easter Sunday," based on the pagan festival) is Pentecost Sunday. On that special, set aside, day in the Christian Liturgical Calendar, what happened on the original Day of Pentecost, which by the way, means "fifty," will be acknowledged and in various ways "observed" by many Christian denominations/groups, Pentecostal and non-Pentecostal. Though its real significance is largely lost on most of its celebrants today, it is a day of commemoration of the original Day of Pentecost that occurred fifty days after the resurrection of Christ when the Holy Spirit was poured out upon 120 disciples who secreted themselves away in a small alcove that became known as, "The Upper Room," awaiting the fulfillment of Jesus' prophecy, "…you shall be baptized with the Holy Spirit not many days from now" (Ac. 1:5).

Christian orthodoxy regards the original Day of Pentecost as the birth day of the Church of Christ. It coincides with the Jewish Feast of Weeks, aka, the Feast of Booths. It was on the last day of this seven-day feast celebrated in a previous year that Jesus first foretold of this outpouring of the Spirit that could not come until after His glorification, meaning, His resurrection and ascension to sit upon His Throne at the right hand of God:

> Now on the last day, the great day of the feast, Jesus stood and cried out, saying, "If anyone is thirsty, let him come to Me and drink. "He who believes in Me, as the Scripture said, 'From his innermost being will flow rivers of living water.'" But this He spoke of the Spirit, whom those who

A Different Gospel—Void of Power 163

believed in Him were to receive; for the Spirit was not yet given, because Jesus was not yet glorified. (Jn. 7:37-39 NASB)

"And when the day of Pentecost had fully come," Luke recounted as rendered in the King James Version, the original Day of Pentecost when the disciples were to receive "the promise of the Father" (Ac. 1:4) with the result that — "ye shall receive POWER, after that the Holy Ghost has come upon you"—transpired thusly:

> When the day of Pentecost had come, they were all together in one place. And suddenly there came from heaven a noise like a violent rushing wind, and it filled the whole house where they were sitting. And there appeared to them tongues as of fire distributing themselves, and they rested on each one of them. And they were all filled with the Holy Spirit and began to speak with other tongues, as the Spirit was giving them utterance. Now there were Jews living in Jerusalem, devout men from every nation under heaven. And when this sound occurred, the crowd came together, and were bewildered because each one of them was hearing them speak in his own language. They were amazed and astonished, saying, "Why, are not all these who are speaking Galileans? "And how is it that we each hear them in our own language to which we were born? "Parthians and Medes and Elamites, and residents of Mesopotamia, Judea and Cappadocia, Pontus and Asia, Phrygia and Pamphylia, Egypt and the districts of Libya around Cyrene, and visitors from Rome, both Jews and proselytes, Cretans and Arabs—we hear them in our own tongues speaking of the mighty deeds of God." And they all continued in amazement and great perplexity, saying to one another, "What does this mean?" But others were mocking and saying, "They are full of sweet wine." But Peter, taking his stand with the eleven, raised his voice and declared to them: "Men of Judea and all you who live in Jerusalem, let this be known to you and give heed to my words. "For these men are not drunk, as you suppose, for it is only the third hour of the day; but this is what was spoken of through the prophet Joel: "And it shall be in the last days,' God says, 'That I will pour forth of my

Spirit on all mankind; and your sons and your daughters shall prophesy, and your young men shall see visions, and your old men shall dream dreams; even on my bondslaves, both men and women, I will in those days pour forth of my Spirit and they shall prophesy. 'And I will grant wonders in the sky above and signs on the earth below, blood, and fire, and vapor of smoke. 'The sun will be turned into darkness and the moon into blood, before the great and glorious day of the Lord shall come. 'And it shall be that everyone who calls on the name of the Lord will be saved.'" (Ac. 2:1-21; NASB; reformatted)

After telling the multitude gathered that what they were witnessing was "THAT" which the prophet Joel had prophesied some eight hundred years or more before, Peter went on to preach one of the most revelatory and conscience-pricking messages ever preached, which resulted in the query of many in the crowd that typifies the cry of millions since, "What must we do to be saved?" which Peter answered by saying,

Repent, and be baptized every one of you in the name of Jesus Christ for the remission of sins, and ye shall receive the gift of the Holy Ghost. For the promise is unto you, and to your children, and to all that are afar off, even as many as the Lord our God shall call. And with many other words did he testify and exhort, saying, Save yourselves from this untoward generation. (Ac. 2:38-40; KJV)

The result of this mighty outpouring of the Spirit was that three thousand in addition to the 120 were miraculously added to the rolls of the Redeemed: "So then, those who had received his word were *baptized*; and that day there were added about *three thousand souls*" (Ac. 2:41; NASB). And, the presumption by most theologians, which is the most reasonable presumption, is that it was with the Holy Spirit, not water, these three-thousand were also *baptized* while the Outpouring was still transpiring in addition to being *infused* with the Holy Spirit in regeneration when they repented and also received the Lord Jesus Christ in salvation, and that as a result these also "began to speak in other tongues as the Spirit gave utterance."

So, the net result of this grandiose deluge of the Spirit from Heaven was that there were now at least 3,120 Spirit-infused and Spirit-baptized believers comprising the Church of Christ on the day of its nativity, and Luke tells us that these initial congregants continued to abide and fellowship together, to be further nourished on the apostles' teaching, and that their numbers continued to grow on a daily basis:

> They were continually devoting themselves to the apostles' teaching and to fellowship, to the breaking of bread and to prayer. Everyone kept feeling a sense of awe; and many wonders and signs were taking place through the apostles. And all those who had believed were together and had all things in common; and they began selling their property and possessions and were sharing them with all, as anyone might have need. Day by day continuing with one mind in the temple, and breaking bread from house to house, they were taking their meals together with gladness and sincerity of heart, praising God and having favor with all the people. *And the Lord was adding to their number day by day those who were being saved.* (Ac. 2:42-47; NASB)

What a glorious start the Church Jesus said He would build was off to after they "received dunamis-power" after that the Holy Spirit came upon them. But, sadly, as we know, things with the First Church did not continue that way very long. In fact, before the First Century ended and the last book of the Bible was written, the Church was already under siege by carnally-minded, non-spirit-baptized CINOs (Christians In Name Only), "false brethren" (2 Cor. 11:26; Gal. 2:4) "enemies of the cross of Christ" (Plp. 3:18), who were well on their way to hijacking the church and gaining political control over it. Jesus even explicitly identified this clique of spiritual gangsters in the revelation He communicated to John, saying that He hated their deeds and disapproved their doctrines or teaching (Rev. 2:6,15). Though historical information of how the Nicolaitans were able to pull off this ecclesiastical *coup-d'éta* is limited, they were able in a relatively short period of time to wrest authority over the Church from the hands of the Apostles where it was placed by the ascending Christ and to bring about a gradual curbing and eventual virtual cessation of the operations of the supernatural "manifestations of the Spirit for the common good" (1 Cor. 12:7) by the saints as well. Bottom line: both the native authority and the power of the Church were effectively abrogated and abolished, and control of the Church was seized by this growing band of First Century Gnostics.

The irrefutable historical fact is that the Nicolaitans' doctrines and deeds, powered by the unseen "deceiving spirits and doctrines of demons" behind them, led to the establishment of a hierarchical leadership system comprised of priests, bishops, archbishops, cardinals, and so on, subjugated ultimately to a singular religious potentate, venerated as the human substantiation of Christ Himself— the Pope. It was this institution of "devoid of the Spirit" (Jude 19) cessationism-promulgating clerics that plunged the Church into the spiritual "black hole" of the Dark Ages– 1,200 long years of spiritual deterioration and devastation from which the Church is still in the process of recovery and restoration today.

The Great Apostasy: The True Beginning of Cessationism

The Dark Ages (313—1517 A.D.) was the collective Church's "Great Apostasy" prophesied by the Apostle Paul:

> But the Spirit explicitly says that in later times some will FALL AWAY FROM THE FAITH paying attention to deceitful spirits and doctrines of demons, by means of the hypocrisy of liars seared in their own conscience as with a branding iron. (1 Tim. 4:1-2)

During this era of pervasive spiritual darkness, the Truth of the Word of God was subverted by humanistic ideologies and vain philosophies (Col. 2:8)—the *"doctrines of demons"* of which Paul forewarned. Eventually, nearly every remnant of Divine Truth, the foundational teachings of the Apostles upon which the Church had been originally established, was distorted, debauched, diluted, degraded, abrogated, and abandoned. The ultimate goal of cessationism—

to take away from the saints the supernatural power resident in the "manifestations of the Spirit," or Charismata, and supplant the native authority for the government and leadership of the Church Jesus is building resident in the Fivefold Ministry Offices—is clearly seen operating throughout the various ages of Church history since the birth of the Church Jesus is building on that first Day of Pentecost when the Holy Spirit was first lavishly poured out upon the Church.

Personally, I believe that the arch-enemy of God and the Church of Christ has been doing all he can to cause by whatever means possible a cessation of the gifts of the Spirit that come through the Baptism of the Spirit ever since they were first poured out on the original Day of Pentecost because he knows full well just how powerful they are against him and his schemes. "The demons also believe, and shudder!" As with most other things, the devil and his cohorts know better and with greater conviction just how powerful that power is that Jesus said believers would receive through the Baptism in the Holy Spirit than believers do! Thus, since that first outpouring he has been waging an all-out, continual war to keep believers from really coming into that power, so to speak, and getting a good hold on it, and using it against the forces of hell to the extent they are able to render spiritual devastation against all the devil is doing in the world, as "the ruler of the world" (Jn. 12:31; 14:30; 16:11) and "the prince and the power of the air" (Eph. 2:2). While some scholars and theologians posit that cessationism began in the 17th or 18th Centuries, it is clear to me that cessationism began in the First Century, from the moment the power of God was poured out upon the Church on the first Day of Pentecost.

My friend, Charles Carrin, whose writings I've quoted several times in this book, wrote a series of outstanding articles refuting cessationism that I published in Spirit Life Magazine (www.spiritlifemag.com), of which I am the founding publisher and editor. The following is his fourth in that series of articles, which he fittingly published in his newsletter a few days before Pentecost 2012. As he did in all the previous articles, he addresses quite a number of additional reasons why cessation theories are absolutely wrong and provides numerous Biblical reasons why Jesus still wants believers to possess the power resident in the Baptism in the Holy Spirit and be possessed by it.

A Different Gospel — Without Power (By Charles Carrin)

> I marvel that you are turning away so soon from Him who called you in the grace of Christ, to **a different gospel**, which is not another; but there are some who trouble you and want to *pervert the gospel of Christ*. But even if we, or an angel from heaven, preach any other gospel to you than what we have preached to you, let him be accursed. As we have said before, so now I say again, if anyone preaches *any other gospel* to you than what you have received, let him be <u>accursed</u>. (Gal. 1:6-9)

Since the beginning of the written Word, Scripture has been the battle-ground for religious wars. In Jesus' day, the Pharisees and Sadducees fought among themselves and with Him about their personal interpretations. If we examine their struggle closely, however, we discover the issue was not so much to protect Scripture as to preserve their personal identities that were dependent on it. The same struggle exists among Christians today. Then, as now, the basic motivation in many theological battles is self-preservation. This is sometimes true of pastors, local congregations, and/or large denominations. In such situations the "Kingdom identity" of the parties involved is totally sacrificed for the sake of protecting their religious ambitions. I do not say this to be unkind. Not at all, I love all Christian bodies and the people in them. It is my desire to help correct problems, not cause them.

While the Pharisees and Sadducees bitterly opposed each other in some issues, they were welded together in their opposition against Jesus. His seeming disrespect for the Sabbath united their anger. Simply stated, the conflict was between their religion and His spirituality. This fact boiled to the surface immediately after He raised Lazarus from the dead. In an urgently-called Council of the Sanhedrin, the Pharisees said of Jesus, "If we let Him alone like this, everyone will believe in Him, and the Romans will come and take away both *our place* and nation" (Jn. 11:48).

The issue of whether or not Jesus was the Messiah was no longer the major concern. The fear was that "everyone will believe in Him;" that is, Jews and Gentiles will universally accept the same spiritual leader, ethnic and religious differences will disappear, personal identities will be lost, and "the Romans will come and take away both our place and (our) nation." This is identical to what happens today when church leaders are confronted with truths that threaten "their place and their nation." Those parts of Scripture that jeopardize denominational identity are quickly anesthetized. It is done theologically, yes, but the result is absolutely the same. The threatening parts are no longer the real threat. The change that is necessitated by new truth is the threat. Even when confronted with truth, religion does not want to convert.

In our day, a major one of these doctrines has the official name of "Cessation Theology." It claims that God withdrew the Holy Spirit's miraculous gifts from the church when the New Testament was fully written. Any passage which speaks of such gifts is now invalid and should be ignored. Consequently, the church is no longer to blame for its failure or the absence of miraculous power. God is to blame. That settles it with some Christians and any further discussion is not tolerated. Anger flares if their opinion is challenged. Even though no one can provide a list of the scriptures that have become invalid, discussion of the subject is not allowed.

What Does Scripture Itself Say?

But, does Scripture say that about itself?

Jesus said: "It is written, man shall not live by bread alone, but by every word that proceedeth out of the mouth of God." (Mat. 4:4)

Jesus said: "Heaven and earth shall pass away but My words will by no means pass away" (Mat. 24:35).

God the Father said: "My Covenant I will not break nor alter the Word that is gone out of my lips" (Psa. 89:34).

Jesus said to the Father: "For I have given to them (the disciples) the words which You have given Me, and they have received them..." (Jn. 17:8).

Peter said: "But the word of the Lord endures forever. Now this is the word which by the gospel was preached to you" (1 Pet. 1:25).

Peter said again: "Knowing this first, that no prophecy of Scripture is of any private interpretation, for prophecy never came by the will of man, but holy men of God spoke as they were moved by the Holy Spirit" (2 Pet. 1:21).

Paul said: "Be diligent...rightly dividing the word of truth" (2 Tim. 2:15).

Paul said again: "All Scripture is given by inspiration of God and is profitable" (2 Tim. 3:16).

Paul said once more: "But even if we, or an angel from heaven, preach any other gospel to you than what we have preached to you, let him be accursed" (Gal. 1:8).

David said: "Forever, O Lord, Your Word is settled in Heaven" (Psa. 119:89).

Do I believe in the inspiration and continuing validity of all New Testament scriptures? Absolutely!

Authentication by Innumerable Recipients

Every church, every pastor, is accountable to God for preaching the full New Covenant message. But we cannot do that without the same power-source on which Jesus depended. On the Day of Ascension, He told the disciples at the Mount of Olives, "John truly baptized with water, but you shall be baptized with the Holy Spirit not many days from now...You shall receive power when the Holy Spirit has come upon you" (Ac. 1:5-6). In a single statement, Jesus connected baptism in the Spirit to the imparting of His power. That wonderful event occurred on the day of Pentecost when 120 disciples in the Upper Room received the blessing.

Scripture carefully explains that others who were not present at Pentecost experienced the same empowering later. That included the Samaritans (Ac. 8:14-17), Saul of Tarsus (Ac. 9:17), the household of Cornelius (Ac. 10:44), and the Ephesians (Ac. 19:1-7). Young Timothy followed the example (2 Tim. 1:6).

Identically, today, multiplied millions around the world have stepped into the Spirit's wondrous baptism.

The Apostle Paul and Spiritual Gifts

The Apostle Paul was born again on the Damascus Road and later received the Holy Spirit's impartation by Ananias' laying-on-of-hands in the Damascus Room. As an Apostle, this man later wrote an 84-verse treatise on spiritual gifts—First Corinthians 12,13,14. His explanation provides the most comprehensive, authoritative information we have on the subject. More importantly, it is the only resource bearing the seal of Divine Authorship. All conflicting opinions, no matter how cherished or long-established, are but human speculation and must be discarded. Scripture is our final, absolute authority.

The Apostle begins his dissertation with the plea: "Now concerning spiritual gifts, brethren, I do not want you to be ignorant" (1 Cor. 12:1). Interestingly, this appeal that we "not be ignorant" appears seven times in the New Testament; once by Peter, six times by Paul. Each time, the request reveals an especially deep concern of the writer. Its appearance here should command the attention of every conscientious believer. The Apostle then proceeds carefully to detail the operation of nine grace-works of the Spirit. These are the direct result of the Spirit's baptism.

Having defended the need and purpose of the gifts, Paul then concludes his discourse with the stirring rebuke, "But if anyone is ignorant, let him be ignorant" (1 Cor. 14:38). In other words, he says, "After this careful explanation of spiritual gifts, if anyone refuses to learn, I have nothing more to say to him. Let him remain illiterate!"

Paul seemingly anticipated that some believers would reject his teaching on miraculous works of the Spirit and added this harsh warning: "If anyone thinks himself to be a prophet or spiritual, let him acknowledge that the things which I write to you are *the commandments of the Lord*" (1 Cor. 14:37). What are the "commandments" of which he speaks? The answer: The Apostolic teachings on spiritual gifts. First Corinthians 12 and 14 speak with God's authority as much as any other of Paul's writings. We are no more at liberty to reject these Biblically mandated instructions than any other commandment of the Lord.

Until recent years, there was probably no other subject about which the Church was more ignorant than that of spiritual gifts. Instead of heeding Paul's instruction, the Church engaged in open warfare against them. This was done in full view of Paul's exhortation that we:

1. "Earnestly desire spiritual gifts" (1 Cor. 12:1).
2. "Pursue love, and desire spiritual gifts, especially that you may prophesy" (1 Cor. 14:1).
3. "Since you are zealous for spiritual gifts, let it be for the edification of the church that you seek to excel" (1 Cor. 14:12).

These admonitions do not indicate the reluctance that typifies the modern church's attitude against spiritual gifts.

There was no such lukewarmness on the part of Paul or the Corinthians. Identically, believers today are encouraged to exercise the gifts for the benefit of everyone:

> But the manifestation of the Spirit is given to each one for the profit of all; for to one is given the word of wisdom through the Spirit, to another the word of knowledge through the same Spirit, to another gifts of healings by the same Spirit, to another faith by the same Spirit, to another gifts of healings by the same Spirit, to another the working of miracles, to another prophecy, to another discerning of spirits, to another different kinds of

A Different Gospel—Void of Power

tongues, to another the interpretation of tongues. But one and the same Spirit works all these things, distributing to each one individually as He wills....But if anyone is ignorant, let him be ignorant. (1 Cor. 12:1;4-11;38)

The argument immediately arises, "These gifts passed away." Paul did not believe that. Nor does the New Testament teach it. In the introduction of his Corinthian letters (29 chapters and longest of all New Testament writings,) Paul exhorted believers to "...Come short in no gift, eagerly waiting for the revelation of our Lord Jesus Christ" (1 Cor. 1:7). In that brief statement, Paul equated the duration of spiritual gifts to be the same length as the Church's waiting for Jesus' return. Examine it for yourself. This is precisely what the Apostle said.

There is probably no greater ignorance in the Church today than of Jesus' offer of the Baptism in the Holy Spirit. What a tragic loss to contemporary Christianity!

The Question of the Reliability of Ancient Manuscripts

The most common attack against Scripture centers upon the reliability of ancient manuscripts and their having been copied numerous times. Since we have only copies and not the original works of the apostolic writers, how can we intelligently defend a book that is thousands of years old? Our defense of the Bible academically can begin with this observation: There are no original copies of any of the following ancient manuscripts, for example:

PLATO: Greek philosopher. His writings are found in a mere seven manuscripts, the oldest copy written twelve hundred years after his death.

ARISTOTLE: Greek philosopher, student of Plato, tutor of Alexander the Great. Only five copies of any one work of Aristotle exist, and none of these were written less than fourteen hundred years after his death.

HERODOTUS: Greek historian. Only eight manuscripts survive; these were copied thirteen hundred years after the original.

EURIPIDES: Greek playwright. Nine manuscripts exist, dated thirteen hundred years after they were first written.

One is immediately struck by the scarcity of copies of these authors and the vast time lapse between the originals and today's reproductions. Yet no one questions their authenticity. Contrast the scarcity of works done by these secular writers to the abundance of New Testament copies. Renowned scholar and professor, Dr. F.F. Bruce, verified approximately 4,000 ancient Greek New Testaments still in existence. Two complete manuscripts are dated less than three hundred years after the original. Most of the New Testament is preserved in copies written less than two hundred years after Jesus. Some existing books were composed about one hundred years after the originals. Part of one book came within a generation of the First Century. Recently, earlier fragments have been found.

If approximately four thousand ancient New Testament manuscripts survived the ravages of time, we are overwhelmed with this question: How large was the original number of others, now lost, that exploded upon the public in the first centuries? What was the motivation—the power—that excited early believers into mass production of this book? The answer, of course, is that the book itself was composed by the Holy Spirit and contained His miraculous anointing. Those who read it became motivated to copy and preserve it.

The Bible's claim to authenticity is totally beyond the reach of all other writers of antiquity. As believers, we stand secure in its reliability.

But, someone asks, why do I need to believe all the New Testament scriptures and to experience spiritual gifts? Here are a few of the many reasons:

1. Jesus said you needed them.
2. Without them, you are an incomplete disciple.

3. Good as you presently are, your personal life will be better with them.
4. You need to be moved out of "carnal" effort into spiritual effort.
5. The Spirit's baptism releases power in your life which can be gained no other way.
6. The baptism will bring astonishing, remarkable information to you personally.
7. The Bible mandates the gifts. Early Christians depended on them. You want all God has for you!

Dare We Edit the Word of God?

A final question: Dare we edit the book that "holy men of God wrote as they were moved by the Holy Spirit?" God forbid that we dare raise our hand against the truth God has spoken! Heaven help us!

I repeat a statement made earlier in this article. I believe it with all my heart.The Apostle Paul's explanation provides the most comprehensive, authoritative information we have on the subject of the Scripture's authenticity. More importantly, it is the only resource bearing the seal of Divine Authorship. All conflicting opinions, no matter how cherished or long-established, are but human speculation and must be discarded. *Scripture is our final, absolute authority!*

Chapter Sixteen
Receiving The Baptism in the Holy Spirit

"...If any man is thirsty, let him come to Me and drink. He who believes in Me, as the Scriptures said, 'From his innermost being will flow rivers of living water.'" But this He spoke of the Spirit, whom those who believed in Him were to receive; for the Spirit was not yet given, because Jesus was not yet glorified. (Jn. 7:37-39)

Then, in Luke 24:49, Jesus is quoted as saying to the early disciples:

"And, behold, I am sending forth the promise of My Father upon you; but you are to stay in the city until you are clothed with power from on high."

And Acts 1:4-5 says that Jesus gathered together the early disciples, and,

He commanded them not to leave Jerusalem, but to *wait* for what the Father had promised, "Which," He said, "you have heard of from Me; for John baptized with water, but you shall be baptized with the Holy Spirit not many days from now."

And then verse 8 says:

"but you will receive power when the Holy Spirit has come upon you; and you shall be My witnesses, both in Jerusalem, and in Judea and Samaria, and to the remotest part of the earth."

Then Acts 2:1-4 says:

And when the Day of Pentecost had come, they were all together in one place. And suddenly there came from Heaven a noise like a violent, rushing wind, and it filled the whole house where they were sitting. And there appeared to them tongues as of fire distributing themselves, and they rested on each one of them. And they were all filled with the

Holy Spirit and began to speak with other tongues, as the Spirit was giving them utterance.

And the verses following indicate that when this sound occurred, the crowd that was gathered together and witnessing this supernatural phenomenal event were bewildered because each one of them was hearing these early disciples, who had been filled with the Holy Ghost, speaking in their own languages.

And verses 12 (and following) say:

> And they continued in amazement and great perplexity, saying to one another, "What does this mean?" But others were mocking and saying, "They are full of sweet wine." But Peter, taking his stand with the eleven, raised his voice, and declared to them: "...these men are not drunk, as you suppose, for it is only the third hour of the day; but *this is (that* which the Prophet Joel had spoken and prophesied so many hundreds of years before): 'And it shall be in the last days,' God says, 'That I will pour forth of My Spirit **upon ALL mankind**; and your sons and your daughters shall prophesy, and your young men shall see visions, and your old men shall dream dreams; even upon My bondslaves, both men and women, I will in those days pour forth of My Spirit and they shall prophesy.'"

And, then, Peter, going on in his momentous sermon on that Day of Pentecost, says, in verse 32:

> This Jesus God raised up again, to which we are all witnesses. Therefore having been exalted to the right hand of God, and having received from the Father the promise of the Holy Spirit, He has poured forth this which you both see and hear. *(Then, picking up in verse 37)* Now when the crowd heard this, they were pierced to the heart, and said to Peter and the rest of the apostles, "Brethren, what shall we do?" And Peter said to them, "Repent and let each of you be baptized in the Name of Jesus Christ for the forgiveness of your sins *(that's talking about water baptism)*. And you shall receive <u>THE GIFT OF THE HOLY SPIRIT</u> *(this refers to the Baptism in the Holy Spirit)*. For the promise is for you and your children, and for all who are far off, as many the Lord our God shall call to Himself."

The Baptism in the Holy Spirit and Fire is available to every believer who will turn to the Lord Jesus Christ, and simply call upon Him, and *ask* Him to receive of this great baptism in the Living Waters of God. As indicated numerous times previously, God desires that ALL believers receive the Baptism in the Holy Spirit with the initial evidence of *tongues*. According to First Corinthians 14, verses 5, 14, and 15, ALL believers should pray and sing in the Spirit, that is, to say *in tongues*. The Apostle Paul tells us in First Corinthians 14:14 that praying in a *tongue* is praying in the *Spirit*. And praying in tongues comes through the Baptism in the Holy Spirit.

The Holy Spirit, through the Apostle Peter, told us, in the passage we looked at previously, that this promise of the Spirit is for *you*, and for your *children*, even for as many as be afar off, meaning those who are yet away from God and alienated from Him by the great chasm of sin and personal sins. All you have to do is come to God, repent of your sin, request His forgiveness that He is so eager to extend, and then *ask* Him for this great Baptism in the Holy Spirit, and Jesus said, "You SHALL receive power after that the Holy Ghost is come upon you."

Why the Baptism in the Holy Spirit and Tongues

Now, in this final segment of teaching, we want to look at some of the many reasons why you would want to receive the Baptism in the Holy Spirit, or the benefits of this great promise of the Father—the Baptism in the Holy Spirit and Fire. Firstly, as I've already indicated, Jesus said we would receive power after that the Holy Ghost has come upon us; and the Amplified Bible says, that we would receive power to testify of Him "with *great effect*." And, certainly, it is *great effect* to testify of Jesus when you are testifying through the power that is demonstrated and manifested through the gifts of the Spirit that are operated through a person who has received of the Baptism in the Holy Spirit, and who steps out in faith, and allows the Holy Spirit to use him or her as a vessel of the power of God.

Secondly, the gifts of the Spirit, especially the gift of *tongues*, are a supernatural sign unto unbelievers, according to First Corinthians 14:22. They are a *sign* to unbelievers, meaning that they are an *indicator*, testifying of the supernatural power of God being manifest through the speaker, as a testimony of the power and presence of God being manifested.

Another reason *tongues* are so important in the lives of believers is that it is genuine *spiritual* prayer, according to First Corinthians 14:14, for there Paul says, "If I pray in a *tongue*, my *spirit* prays." Biblically speaking, the only way to really "pray in the *Spirit*," as it is often referred to, is by praying in *tongues*. The only way we can really know that the Holy Spirit is praying through our human spirit, which is light-years better than us praying on our own out of our finite and flawed intellect, is when we are praying in a *tongue*, according to this verse. Moreover, Romans 8:26 indicates that "praying in *tongues*" is actually the Holy Spirit in the role as the *Paracletos*, as He is called in the Greek— *Paracletos*, the One who comes along side and takes hold with, it literally means. Jesus called Him, "The Helper." The Helper actually is praying or interceding through us when we are praying in the Spirit.

And, in the next verse, we see that another reason for, or benefit of, praying in *tongues* is that the Holy Spirit is praying through us in the perfect will of God, and according to the mind, the thinking, the understanding, the knowledge, the wisdom of God.

So also, Romans 8:1-6 tells us that through *tongues*, when we are praying in *tongues*, the Holy Spirit is helping us with our weakness—our human frailties, our human spiritual inabilities and inadequacies that come from being merely human, or that are inherent in our human essence and estate. The Holy Spirit helps us with those, especially in our spiritual activity of prayer.

And then Jude 20 tells us that we actually "edify" or build ourselves up on our most holy faith when we pray in the Spirit, or the word translated "build up" in the Greek means to "charge up" as a battery is charged up with power. We charge ourselves up with dunamis-power, we build ourselves up, when we pray in the Holy Spirit. For the verse says, "But you, beloved, (that means every Christian—when it says, *"beloved,"* it is referring to every Christian), building yourself up on your most holy faith, *praying in the Holy Spirit."* We are told that "Faith comes by hearing, and hearing by the Word of God (Rom. 10:17)." But we actually *build ourselves up ON* that faith, build our lives up ON that faith, when we *"pray in the Holy Spirit"* (i.e., in tongues). Again, according to First Corinthians 14:14, we are praying in the Spirit when we are praying in *tongues.*

And, then, First Corinthians 14:4 is a correlating passage to that one in Jude 20, for it says, "One who speaks in a *tongue* EDIFIES himself." So, when we speak or pray in a *tongue* we are edifying, building ourselves up, spiritually. And, certainly, in this last hour when we are besieged with so much adversity, troubles, trials, tribulations, perplexities of this world, we have a great need to build ourselves up on our most holy faith, praying in the Holy Spirit, that is, praying in *tongues.*

In First Corinthians 14:2, we see that speaking or praying in *tongues* is direct communication to and with God, in which we are actually speaking *mysteries* in our spirit, but these are *mysteries* that can be interpreted, in some cases, through another gift of the Spirit operating in tandem with tongues, which is the *interpretation of tongues.* And, when we have *tongues* plus *interpretation of tongues,* we then have *prophecy.* Tongues and interpretation of tongues spoken in a public forum is each one half of prophecy. When a public message from God to someone or a group of people is spoken in tongues, it must be coupled with interpretation of tongues in order for the recipients to be able to understand it. But, sometimes, not every time, but sometimes, during our personal prayer and praise in tongues, God will convey a message to us directly that comes in the form of tongues and then the Holy Spirit will follow that message with the interpretation into a language we understand. So, we actually can receive prophecy from God within ourselves (our spirit), as we pray in the Holy Spirit, and then allow the Holy Spirit to give us the interpretation of those tongues that we are praying in. And, oftentimes, God will reveal mysteries to us—things that He wants to communicate to us—direction, guidance, and instruction from the Holy Spirit.

Receive the Baptism in the Holy Spirit Right Now!

Friends, the crowning moment for all this teaching and wooing by the Holy Spirit has now come—reach out right now to receive the Baptism in the Holy Spirit, won't you?! Jesus promised to give the Holy Spirit to everyone who asks Him for it. That's all you have to do—you merely have to *ask* Him to receive of the Holy Spirit. The Bible says, "*Ask*, and you shall *receive*." Indeed, in Luke 11:9-13, He (Jesus) specifically talks about this with regard to the Holy Spirit, the Baptism in the Holy Spirit:

> So I say to you, **ask**, and it will be given to you; *seek*, and you will find; *knock*, and it will be opened unto you. For **everyone** (everyone, everyone, everyone) who asks, receives; and he who seeks, finds; and to him who knocks, it will be opened. Now suppose one of you fathers is asked by his **son** for a **fish**: he will not give him a **snake** instead of a **fish**, will he? *(He is contrasting Satan's kingdom to God's kingdom. Satan's kingdom being represented by a **snake**, and God's kingdom being represented by a **fish**.)* Or if he asks for an **egg**, he will not give him a **scorpion**, will he?" *(Again, the two kingdoms being contrasted; God will not give you something from **Satan's** kingdom when you are asking Him earnestly and diligently to receive something from **His** Kingdom.)* If you then, being evil, know how to give **good gifts** to your children, how much more will your heavenly Father give **the Holy Spirit** to those who **ask** Him?

And, then, in John 7:37-38 and Isaiah 55:1, we see that anyone who is thirsty for the Holy Spirit need only to come to Jesus, and *drink* of the water of the Holy Spirit, that is, receive it by *faith*. It's truly just that easy. Out of fear, or unbelief, or self-condemnation, people are often so intimidated about merely asking Jesus for the Baptism in the Holy

Spirit, but it really is as simple as drinking from a glass of water! He's not holding back. He's eager to baptize you in the Spirit right now—whenever you ask Him!

Friend, right now I want to help you to receive the Baptism in the Holy Spirit. And, you know, you can!—right where you are right now. If you are a believer in the Lord Jesus Christ, and you have been *regenerated* by the Holy Spirit coming to live on the inside of you, to take up residence on the inside of you, in your heart, you are a candidate for the Baptism in the Holy Spirit. This is what you have been looking for! This is what you have a need for! This is what you have been lacking—the *power of God*, operating in your life.

It is so simple! All you need to do is to ask Jesus, and then simply *drink in* the Holy Spirit. If you earnestly desire to be totally immersed in the Rivers of Living Water of the Holy Spirit, you can be immersed in those Waters right now, wherever you are at this moment!

Lift both hands to Heaven, and pray this prayer with me; say it out loud with me right now. Go ahead!

Dear Lord Jesus, I have believed upon You as my Lord and Savior, and the Holy Spirit already lives within me. I know I am already saved. But, John the Baptist testified You were the Baptizer in the Holy Spirit! I ask You now to baptize me in the Holy Spirit, and clothe me with power from on High. I receive this Baptism now by faith.

Now, friend, to drink—drink out of a glass of water—you must open your mouth. So open your mouth right now, get ready to drink. Jesus said, if you are thirsty, come and ask Him, and drink. Now take in a deep breath right now, drink in the Breath of the Holy Spirit; receive by faith.

Father, I ask You in Jesus' Name that you baptize these readers and listeners with the Baptism in the Holy Ghost and Fire!

Now, go ahead, beloved, drink in the Holy Spirit—take three deep breaths right now as if you are drinking water—

drink in the Spirit, the Breath of God!

Oh, Holy Spirit, fall upon them now as you fell upon the Gentile believers gathered at Cornelius' house, I pray, in Jesus' Name!

Now just receive the Holy Spirit's baptism by faith; it is not by works. It comes just the same way that you got saved—you received Jesus by *faith*—now receive the Baptism in the Holy Spirit by *faith*. You will begin to sense a bubbling forth, a sensation from your innermost being, somewhere in the region of your belly, for Jesus said, "out of your *belly* shall flow rivers of living water." For that is where your human spirit is located, somewhere behind your belly.

Open your mouth, begin singing the praises of God, begin to speak the praises of God in the utterances that the Holy Spirit gives you from within. You must *allow* Him to use your *tongue*. Surrender your *tongue* to Him, right now. Don't be concerned if only a few sounds that you do not understand come forth initially. Just speak them forth in faith, abandoning pride and self-consciousness. Remember: tongues are words in languages *you* do not understand, but *God does*!

A Few Words of Instruction for After You Have Received the Spirit-Baptism

Now let me give you a few words of instruction.

EXERCISE your *prayer language* whenever possible and it will continue to develop. It is like anything else, the more you use it, the more you will receive. If you do not use it, you will lose it, eventually—not the Holy Spirit, but this ability to speak in languages that He gives you by the supernatural power of God, because Satan comes immediately to steal the word that has been sown in your heart (cf., Mk. 4:15). The more you use it—i.e., speak in tongues—the more you will know by faith that it is real and Satan will not be able to cause you to doubt it.

RESIST the lies of the devil (Jas. 4:7), and his attempts to steal from you what you have received from God, for He will surely come and try to steal it from you. But you have to *resist* his attempts to steal it, and know that you have received something *good* from God (Jas. 1:16-17). You have received the true *gift* of the Holy Spirit from God, for Jesus is the Baptizer in the Holy Ghost and Fire!

CONNECT and fellowship with believers of "like precious faith" (2 Pet. 1:1; KJV) who also believe in and have received the Baptism in the Holy Spirit, and who therefore will not be constantly trying to tell you all kinds of things contrary to what the Word of God says about it. Just being around people who believe as you do exposes you to an atmosphere of *belief* as opposed to *unbelief*. To do this, if you have been fellowshipping and having relationships with people who do not believe in the Baptism of the Holy Spirit and the supernatural gifts that are distributed by the Holy Spirit, you will have to separate yourself from them, unfortunately [whenever practicable and prudent; at least spiritually, if physically is not a practical option] (cf., 2 Cor. 6:14-18). If you do not separate yourself from people who do not espouse what you espouse, i.e., teaching in agreement with the Word of God, you are giving Satan legal right and opportunity to subject you to constant bombardment with schemes and devices aimed at eroding your faith over time. Don't give him any place in your life (Eph. 4:27)!

* * * * *

Having arrived at our final destination and our journey ended, I want to say I praise God for the mighty Baptism in the Holy Ghost and Fire! Moreover, it is a safe assumption, considering the status quo across the vast landscape of Christendom in this hour, that I can correctly echo the words of the Apostle Paul in saying that I praise God that I speak in tongues more than most of those reading and hearing these words right now. And, THAT, as far as I am concerned, in the final analysis, is the most convincing and uncontestable response of all to the false claims of all the cessationists who stubbornly allege that all the gifts of the Spirit, tongues included, "passed away" ages ago with the death of the last remaining Apostle of the Lamb, or the First Century church—that for the last nearly four complete decades I personally have spoken in tongues profusely and repeatedly, ever since the very moment the Holy Spirit fell upon me about four months after surrendering my heart, life, and sinfulness, unto my personal Lord, Master, and Savior, Jesus Christ.

Trying to now convince me, after nearly 40 years of not only speaking in tongues but also operating in all nine of the gifts of the Spirit as He willed, as well as, at times, in all five of the Ministry Gifts as He anointed me, that tongues are not for today, would be like trying to convince me that after 65 years of life I need to go back into my mother's womb and not be physically born. To invoke a saying, "The genie is already out of the bottle!" For me, it's too late for convincing! To me, the whole argument is ludicrous, completely illogical, and senseless!

Again, I praise God Almighty for the indescribable gift of the Baptism in the Holy Ghost and Fire, and all the supernatural gifts of which I have been a recipient and beneficiary over these past four decades!

One final thought that I will share is that, based on all that has been established from Scripture in this volume regarding the workings of the Holy Spirit, the Third Member of the Godhead, all believers, from the pulpit to the pew, would do well to heed the Spirit's warning: "Do not quench the Spirit. Despise not prophesyings" (1Thes. 5:19-20). For, to do so will assuredly engender consequences, either in this life or the life to come, and more than likely, both! "So then **each one of us** will give an account of himself to God" (Rom. 14:12).

Believers, don't let any minister deprive you of the empowerment of the Spirit that comes through the Baptism in the Holy Spirit! Ministers, be sure your teaching aligns with Scripture, for teachers incur a stricter judgment (Jas. 3:1)!

Charismatic Captivation

Authoritarian Abuse & Psychological Enslavement in Neo-Pentecostal Churches

ISBN 978-1-887915-00-7
Dr. Steven Lambert

Multitudes of sincere and trusting believers in Charismatic and other Neo-Pentecostal churches are unaware victims of "Charismatic Captivation," ensnared in the virtually invisible web of authoritarian abuse, psychological enslavement, and self-aggrandizing exploitation by church leaders.

Charismatic Captivation is an expose' of widespread hyper-authoritarianism in many segments of the Church-at-large.

It explains how to recognize the signs and symptoms of authoritarian abuse, as well how victims can attain liberation from this insidious "snare of the trapper," recovery from the psychological trauma, and restoration from the spiritual damage they've experienced. Perhaps the most ***comprehensive*** book ever written on the subject, but unquestionably the most ***controversial*** ever written on the matter of authoritarian abuse, especially because it is written from the insider's perspective of a Charismatic minister.

"Shocking! Horrifying! A real eye-opener! Incredible!"—are some common reactions of readers.

Read more at: http://www.charismatic-captivation.com.

Charismatic Control

Witchcraft in Neo-Pentecostal Churches

ISBN 978-1-887915-01-4
Dr. Steven Lambert

A powerful booklet-size adaptation of the "big book"— *Charismatic Captivation*.

This condensed version was published as a tool to assist believers in ministering to loved ones and friends to help them find freedom from the profound spiritual impact and psychological trauma of authoritarian abuse.

It contains *"The Fifteen Common Control Mechanisms,"* as well as *33 Signs of Spiritual Abuse* employed by dominating and controlling ministries and church-groups, along with other vital information for recognizing this abominable form of abuse not included in the "big book."

The booklet's central theme is demonstrating from Scripture that this kind of personal predominance by spiritual leaders is in fact **witchcraft** of the highest order!

As a Christian counselor, the author addresses the true nature of witchcraft and the severe impact it can have on virutually every aspect of its victims' lives.

Read more at: http://www.charismatic-captivation.com.

ISBN 978-1-887915-02-1
Dr. Steven Lambert

The Mystery of the Kingdom

Bearing Kingdom Fruit

Read more at:
RealTruthPublications.Com

The Mystery of the Kingdom is a virtual *Christianity 101*, and is must-reading for every believer! It puts the entire "big picture" of the Christian experience and life into proper perspective. Its message is based on the Paramount Parable—The Parable of the Sower. Jesus Himself said this was most important of all His parables, and the book explains why that is so. He also said that inherent within the parable were "the mysteries of the kingdom"—the spiritually-appraised "secrets" of how the entire Kingdom of God operates.

The four categories of hearers of the Word of God and their Eternal destiny is the central theme of both the parable and the book. Everyone who has ever heard the Gospel of Christ is represented by one of the categories. All hearers determine their own future and eternal destiny by their response to the Seed that has been sown in the soil of their hearts. Jesus declared that any tree (believer) that does not eventually bear forth kingdom fruit would be cut down and thrown into the fire!

The Mystery of the Kingdom tells how to bring forth Kingdom fruit in one's own life and thus avert eternal judgment and eternal separation from God!

The PROPHETIC GIFTS & OFFICE
—A Biblical Perspective

Read more at:
RealTruthPublications.Com

ISBN 1-887915-03-6
Dr. Steven Lambert

In 1986, the Lord declared through prophetic utterance in a gathering of prophets and prophetic people that He was at that time restoring the prophetic gifts and office in the Church.

The Restoration of the Prophetic Gifts and Office is one of the most comprehensive volumes exclusively addressing the matter of the prophetic gifts and office published to date.

The manual chronicles in great detail the Biblical foundation of the prophetic gifts and office, how the prophetic was abbrogated during church history, its recent restoration, and its validity and role in the Church today and the future.

The teaching contained in this volume is based on not only extensive research of Church history and painstaking study of Scripture, but also on the author's more than twenty years of experience in prophetic ministry.

Laymen and ministers alike have been greatly enlightened by this virtual encyclopedia of the prophetic realm.

An entire course that includes the text, audio tapes, exam, and Certificate of Completion is also available. Order today!

DELIVERANCE from DEMONIC POWERS

STEVEN LAMBERT

ISBN 978-1-887915-09-0
Dr. Steven Lambert

Read more at:
RealTruthPublications.Com

A comprehensive but concise book on the misunderstood and much maligned matter of deliverance from demonic powers (also known as, "exorcism").

This volume was written for the purpose of telling the straightforward, Scriptural *"Real Truth"* about demonization, both for those who suspect they or someone they love needs deliverance, as well as those who have a heart and calling to help others to be set free from demonic influence.

The book addresses the salient issues of deliverance from a theological perspective without all the superfluous anecdotal "fluff" and psychology-based theories and therapies contained in most other books on the topic. It answers the most frequently asked questions about the dynamics of how demonization occurs and how to be delivered.

This guide is must-reading for all true believers who are sick and tired of being sick and tired and of standing idly by, enduring the constant and continuous confluence of chaos, confusion, contention, and corruption in their own life, their relationships and interrelations with others, and in the lives of their loved ones.

ABOUT THE AUTHOR

DR. STEVEN LAMBERT has been ministering the Gospel of Jesus Christ as an ordained minister since 1976, serving as a pastor, prophet, teacher, conference speaker, and a Christian counselor. He is a Doctoral Diplomate Board Certified Christian Therapist, and holds several earned theological degrees. He also ministers as an apostolic prophet to help establish existing churches and plant new ones.

He also serves as the Overseer of *Ephesians Four Network* (ephesiansfour.net), an international fellowship of Fivefold Ministers relating and colaboring for common purposes, and its subsidiary, *Ephesians Four Network of Deliverance Counselors* (efndc.ephesiansfour.net).

Dr. Lambert is the author of a number of books, booklets, Bible college courses, and other teaching materials (catalog at realtruthpublications.com), as well as the publisher of an online magazine, *Spirit Life Magazine* (spiritlifemag.com), which is dedicated to extolling, elucidating, and experiencing Life in the Spirit.

Dr. Lambert speaks on the topic of authoritarian abuse and many other vital apostolic/prophetic topics in churches, conferences, and other venues. His bio and scheduling information are available on the ministry website at: www.slm.org. Email booking inquiries to: booking@slm.org.

www.ingramcontent.com/pod-product-compliance
Lightning Source LLC
Chambersburg PA
CBHW022358040426
42450CB00005B/235